WELBY O'BRIEN

REVISED EDITION

LOVE OUR VETS

Restoring Hope for Families of Veterans

with PTSD

"...a unique and valuable resource...
practical and emotional support to countless loved ones of veterans."
Suzanne Best, Ph.D. Co-author of *Courage After Fire*

"Thank you to all who contributed to this wonderful book. The question-answer format and inclusion of real stories and experiences makes *Love Our Vets* a unique and valuable resource that I'm certain will provide both practical and emotional support to countless loved ones of veterans."

SUZANNE BEST, PHD, CO-AUTHOR OF *COURAGE AFTER FIRE*

"Couldn't put this book down! Powerful. Loved the humor too. What a read! We finally have a book that deals with the reality, courage, faith, and real hope for loved ones of PTSD survivors."

LINDA WHITE, WIFE OF A VIETNAM VETERAN

"*Love Our Vets* offers insight not found in previous publications that I have read. Being a Vietnam vet diagnosed with the disorder, I can appreciate Welby's call for support from those closest to the problem. Those that love us!"

JERRY W. KEEN, COMMAND MASTER CHIEF, USN (RET); CHAIRMAN, CLARK COUNTY VETERANS ASSISTANCE CENTER

"For those of us under the stress of being caregiver to a loved one who suffers from PTSD, Welby provides a priceless resource of strength. This insightful book offers a place to start rebuilding a spiritual foundation for our own strength and healing, and a better relationship with our PTSD loved one."

CHERYL, MOTHER OF AN AFGHANISTAN VETERAN

"I loved it! I found myself laughing one minute and crying the next! I am amazed and relieved that others are going through the same trials as we are. I do not feel as alone as I did before. I loved reading some of the stories to him, and I could see a bit of relief in him, knowing that he is not the only one acting the way he does and that he is not alone as well. We found ourselves talking about things that have happened. I wholeheartedly recommend this book to anyone with a loved one who is a post-war vet! It is a freeing feeling, knowing that we are not alone, and I plan on reading the book again and again when I feel down and discouraged. *Love Our Vets* has given me so many insights on his actions and tools to help ease and get through the hard times."

DANIELLE K, WIFE OF IRAQ VETERAN

"This is the best book on PTSD and vets I've ever read. Anyone who works with vets, or is related to a vet, needs this book. You won't regret it. As a professor, this book is definitely at the top of my reading list on PTSD. Welby O'Brien is honest, insightful, and incredibly compassionate. Gutsy and sensitive. Absolutely fantastic!"

DR. STEVE STEPHENS, PH.D., AUTHOR;
PSYCHOLOGIST SPECIALIZING IN TRAUMA ISSUES; POST-GRAD PROFESSOR

"I've picked up countless books about PTSD, thumbed through them, and thrown them down. I'm so glad to know there are *real people*, going through the same *reality* out there, and I'm not alone. And there is real help and real advice. Thank you!"

RENEE, LOVED ONE OF A PTSD VETERAN

"*Love Our Vets* is by far the best book I have ever read about PTSD!"

VIETNAM VETERAN AND CHAIRMAN OF VET CENTER

"I barely made it through the first few pages, crying. Someone understands!"

PTSD SURVIVOR

"I have read *Love Our Vets* from cover-to-cover and wholeheartedly endorse this book as an excellent resource for both family members of veterans and for veterans/active military members themselves."

DREW DEATON, PRESIDENT & CEO
HONOR THE SACRIFICE, WWW.HONOR-THE-SACRIFICE.ORG

"It was a life saver, and I am grateful beyond words for what it has meant to me!"

WIFE OF COMBAT VETERAN

"Thank you for the amazing book *Love Our Vets*. It is an inspiration!"

ELA, SPOUSE OF ACTIVE-DUTY SERVICE MEMBER

"Thank you, Welby, for writing a wonderful, inspiring, helpful book. I'm loving every word!"

MARINE MOMMA @ SUPPORT OUR MILITARY HEROES

"Sensitive and profoundly useful."

VA CHAPLAIN

"To anyone who is needing encouragement and support, this book is a lifesaver! Reading *Love Our Vets* is paying off in dividends, not only in my caregiver role with veterans, but also in healing my own wounds and learning new ways to manage my own fears and challenges."

LAURA, VETERAN AND PTSD SURVIVOR

"Amazing resource for caregivers... 5 stars!"

HAHNA LEAH

"For anyone who is working with someone who is in a relationship to a veteran with PTSD, this will be a most helpful book that they can put into the hands of the counselee."

MILITARY CHAPLAIN ROY W. LUDLOW

"We received your book are stuck on it! The first few pages had so much information and hope for families it has been hard to put it down. Thank you for your support, and we will surely be telling everyone to check out this book. It is beyond amazing!"

GOLD STAR FAMILY OF MARINE LCPL NATHANIEL 'NATE' SCHULTZ
4/30/91 KIA 8/21/10 "UNTIL EVERY TROOP COMES HOME"

"*Wow*, where have you been? A lot of the PTSD books and information do a good job of addressing the vet, but the spouse (a key figure in recovery), at least mine, feels a little left out—in the dark, so to speak. Thank you!"

DR. BOB LANTRIP, POINTMAN OUTPOST LEADER, SEMPER FI

"I found myself laughing, crying, and empathizing with the problems our returning vets deal with. These brave men and women need our thanks, our help, and perhaps most of all our gratitude for our ability to live in freedom when the price they pay and continue to pay is so dear."

GAIL WELBORN, BOOK REVIEWER

"I think it's the best book I have ever read. I am very impressed!"

REBECCA McCOY, WWW.ASPOUSESSTORYPTSD.COM

"This is an amazing resource! Sometimes the caretakers and loved ones get pushed under the rug. This book is for us! Great stories to help you know that you are not alone, and resources we could all use."

HAYLEY KOLB

"No one ever gave me anything for my wife or family. *Thank you!*"

A GRATEFUL VETERAN

WELBY O'BRIEN

LOVE OUR VETS

RESTORING HOPE FOR FAMILIES OF VETERANS
with PTSD

Deep River
B O O K S

NOTE: Do not use the information in this book to diagnose or treat any condition without consulting a qualified health or mental health care provider.

Published by
Deep River Books
Sisters, Oregon
www.deepriverbooks.com

ISBN (Revised Edition)–9781940269597

Library of Congress: 2012946611

Cover design by David Litwin, PureFusion Media

Printed in the United States of America

DEDICATION

To Frank, the love of my life and hero of my heart.
I thank God for the privilege of journeying together
through this life with you.

FOREWORD

This is not a book about theory or academic ideas from experts. It is grassroots, practical advice from wives and loved ones who are struggling to make sense out of their veteran's PTSD. Most of us don't take hard situations as teaching moments in our life. Instead we run and we want to escape. We can easily become addicted to anything that will ease our pain and discomfort.

Here is a book for PTSD spouses, families, and all loved ones, that is far more than just a survival guide. It is a challenge to grow and thrive by embracing the difficult questions that come from living with PTSD. It is humble, offering no magical or pat answers. Just practical and authentic wisdom learned through trial and error.

Full of real questions and real answers, this book comes out of the lives and experiences of veterans' wives, partners, and all loved ones who are learning a day at a time to live and thrive in spite of PTSD.

ERIC E. MUELLER, PH.D., CLINICAL PSYCHOLOGIST

CONTENTS

It takes an exceptional person to love a warrior, especially a warrior whose war will never cease.

Part Three – REFLECT – Our Wisdom—143

INTRODUCTION

This book is not a treatise on PTSD, nor an attempt to fix it. There are excellent resources on this disorder from as far back as the first wars, continuing to modern breakthroughs every day. Neither is it a marriage/relationship manual. (I would never attempt to write either!) The purpose of this book is to provide comfort, encouragement, and practical help for spouses, families, and all other loved ones of veterans with PTSD. Their hearts of gold have drawn us to them, and our lives are dedicated to loving them. The more loved ones of veterans I meet, the more I see that those who are drawn to them also have hearts of gold. I wonder if pain is the seed that turns hearts into gold ...

This book is down-to-earth. Real. So real you may see yourself. My guess is that your story is much like mine. We share a lot in common. And how perplexing it is that no one else seems to get it! We struggle with fear, loneliness, anxiety, and sleepless nights. We question our sanity and have regular hormone checkups. We don't dare tell anyone that we wonder if we made a mistake. And we feel ashamed at the fleeting thoughts of how much simpler life would be without PTSD.

You are not alone. You share with many others, with all of us in a relationship of some kind with our vets, journeying down the same path. As you read, you will see that the personal experiences shared in this book come from many people just like you—including me. All names are fictitious but the accounts are authentic. Many who have often been tempted to throw in the towel—and a few who have. But even more who grow stronger each day, not in spite of PTSD but because of it. The faith and love that has kept them from falling apart, held them up, and comforted and strengthened them are available to all of us. We need each other. It is in sharing the struggles and growth, pain and healing, and tears and joys that encourages us to love our vets even more. There is no greater reward.

PART ONE

REAFFIRM

Our Questions

What is your dream? We all want something. We long for it. Always have.

What do you want—really want? What makes your heart ache, and what drives you to keep going? I have always longed for an enduring and fulfilling marriage. I want what I see in the movies. I want the honeymoon to last forever.

Well, now that I am all grown up and have experienced a failed marriage, as well as several years of a happy one, my dream is now subject to the confines of reality. We all know that no matter how wonderful the marriage, the honeymoon does not last forever. That is just a fact of human nature. But we do know that really great, successful, and fulfilling marriages are possible. But is that true for those with PTSD? All of us who are married to, or in a relationship with, a vet with PTSD are asking, "Is it possible for us to have a happy and fulfilling relationship?"

What about those who are related in other ways to their veteran? Parents, siblings, children, friends, partners, and even coworkers. We all desire positive relationships with those we care about. Is there hope in all the craziness?

After many years of wrestling with that question and seeking the perfect key, I finally realize it does not exist. There is no easy way. No magic formula. But what I have found in my own life and the lives of those around me is a principle that seems to be consistent. For all relationships.

The most successful marriages and healthiest individuals seem to have more of this than those who don't. Amazingly simple. But also a continuous goal. It is in the day-to-day living that we have the opportunities to experience the blessings of these two treasures: faith and love—shown by actions, and not dependent on feelings.

Faith is connection with God; love is connection with others. It is in connecting that healing and growth triumph. The comfort and closeness heals and nourishes. Ultimately, it is faith and love that provide the lifeline we so desperately need. The pain and struggles do not go away. But where there is comfort there is hope. Truly we can find hope and practical help for ourselves personally and for our relationships.

For the remainder of this book, I've chosen to use male pronouns in the interest of consistency. Please know that when I refer to "he" or "him," these same strategies and words of encouragement apply if your brave loved one happens to be female. Men or women—this devastating disorder doesn't play favorites.

The following pages contain a gold mine of practical help and hope for all who care for a veteran with PTSD. Although my own experience is in the context of marriage to a Vietnam veteran, the wisdom shared applies to all from all conflicts. Your loved one may even still be serving in the military. My hope is that this book will support and encourage *all of you* who struggle to love the vet in your life who has PTSD. You are the wives, the husbands, the parents, the children, and the dear friends who have made a courageous commitment to love your vet as well as humanly possible. He or she is your hero, but you are a hero too.

1. What is PTSD?

Posttraumatic Stress Disorder can occur as a result of exposure to a severe trauma. According to the Mayo Clinic, it is a "mental health condition that's triggered by a terrifying event." Wikipedia defines it as a "severe anxiety disorder that can develop after exposure to any event that results in psychological trauma. This event may involve the threat of death to oneself or to someone else, or to one's own or someone else's physical, sexual, or psychological integrity, overwhelming the individual's ability to cope." It may be an automobile accident, an assault, the tragic loss of a loved one, witnessing a horrific event, or anything that is horrible and shocking.

From the beginning of civilization, PTSD has haunted its victims and their loved ones. Throughout history it has had other names, such as "battle fatigue," "soldier's heart," and "shell shock." Currently, advocates are trying to drop the "D" and just call it "Posttraumatic Stress" in an effort to reduce the stigma that may be attached.

Up until the last few decades, PTSD went relatively undiagnosed and unacknowledged. Now we know better. It is a serious problem affecting many of our men and women, particularly those who have experienced combat. The atrocities our veterans experienced are often too horrendous to talk about—and in many cases, are locked away "safely" in the deepest parts of their memory.

There are many ways to describe PTSD and the effect it has. Here is one simple description: Posttraumatic Stress Disorder can affect anyone (not just military personnel). The whole person gets permanently locked into emergency mode after a horrific experience. For the rest of their lives, they live as if the original trauma or an impending crisis could strike at any moment. It overwhelms their ability to cope, so when something triggers them back into survival mode, they have no reserve with which to handle it.

Visualize a reserve tank of coping skills for stress. Most people have a ready supply on hand for emergencies. PTSD, however, uses about ninety-five percent of the tank's reserves, due to the brain operating in impending crisis mode at all times. The remaining five percent is all they have to handle real stress. Therefore, when something triggers them, they have no reserve with which to handle it in a healthy way. Some terms used are that they get "triggered," "activated," or "hijacked."

PTSD affects millions just in the United States alone, along with all those who love them and live with them.

It is not a chosen situation, an illness, or a temporary condition, nor is it 100% curable. People who struggle with it are not crazy, weak, failures, or bad people, nor are they without help and hope.

Because the trauma can impact them on every level (physically, emotionally, mentally, and spiritually), the manifestations are quite extensive. Some of the typical symptoms may include flashbacks, intrusive thoughts of the trauma, avoidance, numbing, putting up walls, withdrawing, hypervigilance, irritability, being easily startled, memory blocks, sudden bursts of anger or other emotions, difficulty sleeping, nightmares, fear, depression, anxiety, substance abuse and other addictive behaviors, difficulty holding a job, relationship problems, and sometimes even suicide. They are people who are reacting normally to an abnormal experience.

The PTSD may be here to stay, but the good news is that they can learn to thrive again!

I encourage everyone to take advantage of every opportunity to learn more about PTSD and its effects. It is also related to Traumatic Brain Injury. Include TBI in your research also. We are fortunate to have an abundance of resources, including classes, the VA, books, support groups, the internet, and those who live it firsthand. We are continually updating our website as new resources and information become available. www.LoveOurVets.org

✍

2.   Can his PTSD affect me?

Hard as we try to not let it, it does. It is inevitable for two reasons. First, ever notice that when two people live together and are close on any level, they can't help but rub off on each other? Conscious and subconsciously we affect each other. This goes for both positive and negative (sorry...I was hoping to just give out good news today).

The other reason we are affected by their PTSD is the nature of the disorder. Having lived with it ourselves, we do not need to be psychologists to know that those around are indeed impacted. The effects vary because each situation and each person is unique. However, the following may be considered typical when living with a PTSD vet: anxiety, fear, anger, mood-matching, taking on their obsessive-compulsive behaviors, trying too hard to fix them, being diligent to avoid anything that triggers them, sleep disturbances and deprivation, depression, isolation, avoidance, mood swings, hyper-vigilance (sound like someone you know?), negativity, wanting to run away, wanting to throw in the towel, wondering if you made a mistake, feeling trapped, entertaining thoughts of suicide, filling your life with busy activities to distract, finding yourself trying to try harder, wishing someone understood, dreading going to sleep at night and dreading getting up in the morning, feeling terribly alone, feeling unloved, experiencing road rage, getting triggered yourself, trying really hard to figure things out, seeing things with a distorted perspective, poor self-esteem, feeling irritable, struggling with food or other comfort addictions, feeling callused with walls up, wondering when you stopped living, feeling hopeless, questioning your faith, feeling drained and exhausted—and the list goes on.

It has been said that there is such a thing as secondary PTSD. Similar to getting cancer from second-hand smoke. It has also been labeled "vicarious trauma." As loving, caring individuals, we have over time been exposed indirectly to their trauma. It will affect us on every level: emotionally, physically, spiritually, and psychologically.

Camille's vet came home from a lunch meeting with his fellow veterans. At the restaurant, a lady had come up to them and started bragging about what she did to help the other side during the war. The enemy! He got so enraged (understandably so!) he stormed out and sped home. All the rest of that day he spilled his anger on her. Trying to be a good wife and to be supportive, she listened. That night she could not sleep. It was an awful night.

The following day, she was perplexed (and exhausted), trying to figure out why she was such a wreck. At her next visit to her counselor, he explained what is called "limbic contagion." Like vicarious trauma, the limbic system (part of the brain) gets activated under acute stress. In severe cases, this leads to PTSD. For those of us who live with it, we can indeed be affected by it. Camille was experiencing her husband's PTSD. His encounter at the restaurant put him back in the war. To him and his brain he was literally there. Again. In battle. Fighting to survive against the enemy. What she had not realized was that she was there as well.

It will affect me when he is triggered. The question is not how to keep it from affecting me, but *how is it affecting me*? My key lies in tuning in to what is going on inside of me—learning to be more attentive to my needs and internal signals, and not just working hard to try to make it all go away. Here is some of the wisdom from Camille's journal that she gleaned from her counselor:

"When I feel something is wrong, tune in to it. Name it. Feel it and experience it. Feel the sensation (stomach, neck, heart, short breaths, etc.). Ask myself: What part of my body is not right at this moment? For me, it usually is that I stop breathing or breathe shallowly and am stooped over forward. Hunched. Tight neck. I feel like crying inside. Stay with it. Don't rush or try to fix it. Breathe!!!!!!!!! It may move. Do a body-scan mentally. Slowly go from top of my head to the bottom of my toes and feel every sensation. No analyzing. Just notice the sensations. Then, still relaxing, 'go' to a place where I love to be. A happy place where I can feel good, and find comfort.

"My goal is not to not have it affect me but to *be aware of the effect*. *Tune in!* Feel it and release it. Not being aware of it creates the tension that is destructive. Differentiate and acknowledge. His pain. His trauma. My pain. My trauma. Talk about it. As I take care of me and feel and communicate, it helps him. Do not do it only in order to help him, but know that it will benefit him."

As loved ones, our challenge, along with Camille, is how do we get ourselves back to where we are not hijacked emotionally? Learn to calm ourselves. We need to learn how to regulate our emotions by indentifying them and getting ourselves back to a place where we can think. Clearly.

Soundly. Our safety skills are to regulate us, not to stop others from affecting us. Our theme should be "feel; don't fix." I like to think of it in three steps:

1. Feel my body: Where do I feel it physically?
2. Feel my emotion: Name it. "I feel ticked off."

Pause here as long as you want. Take time. Don't rush to figure or fix.

3. Feel my need: What do I need right now that would nurture and comfort me in a healthy way?

Whatever labels one may select, the bottom line is that we are indeed affected. No question about it. But there is hope. Don't stop here. Just know you are not alone. You are going in the right direction with people who care and understand.

☙

3. Is there a cure or can it improve?

Sort of, and possibly. (I could have said, "Of course. Take this green pill and in six days everything will be super duper." Wouldn't that be nice?) We all wish we had a definitive answer to this age old question! And as the great debate continues, millions of vets and their loved ones struggle with the relentless battles of posttraumatic stress. Is there hope or not?

At first, I thought we were stuck. Forever. Just deal with it. And unfortunately that is what many people say. But now that I have personally experienced growth and healing and have seen it in others, I am excited to say, "Yes!" There are all sorts of possibilities.

Our vets we love will never totally get over it. Even in the best cases, the PTSD will always be lurking inside them. But, together, we can learn how to handle it better and how to have a healthy relationship in spite of it.

A brave young veteran recently shared with me that she has it from Iraq, her father had it from Vietnam, and her grandfather from WWII. He may have been one of many who was locked up in an asylum and tortured with shock "therapy." Have we come a long way since then? Absolutely! Do we still have a long way to go! Unequivocally!

The good news is that there are many very effective therapies available today that are resulting in significant improvements in those with PTSD. In some cases, the symptoms of PTSD appear to totally subside. Numerous variables combine to determine what treatments will benefit individuals and to what degree. And new research and developments continue to emerge.

The hard news is that no matter how effective the treatment, or how wide the possible range of recovery, it will never be able to take away the fact that a person experienced the trauma in the first place. The trauma itself can never be erased. So in that sense, the posttraumatic stress will never be 100% cured.

However, the effects of the trauma can be reduced so they no longer control one's life 24/7. That is where our efforts as loved ones, caregivers, supporters, and therapists are primarily focused: minimally, to help those who struggle to manage the symptoms. We encourage them to develop as many coping skills and personal support systems as possible. As we say at Love Our Vets, "They can learn to thrive again!"

I recently received a message from a veteran's loved one about the PTSD not being 100% curable. "I am a fixer and this I can't fix! It scares me, especially for all of our loved ones returning from war. I am so very sad for this."

My reply to her was, "We cannot *fix*, but we *do* have hope! There is a lot that *can* be done to help those with PTSD. I know. I live it!"

Without hope, we cease to thrive. But at the same time, we have to be cautious not to promise a total cure we do not possess. Here are my thoughts on what *can* be done:

1. Accept that there is no quick or easy fix.
2. Keep an open mind, but proceed with open eyes.

3. Be willing to do some hard or uncomfortable work.
4. Connect regularly to a good support network.
5. Stay current on PTSD therapies, resources, and developments.
6. Surround yourself with people who care, and hold on tightly to those you love.

DEBBIE SHARES A LITTLE HOPE FROM HER LIFE:

"When we first learned about PTSD, all I spent my energy on was analyzing and trying to understand it all. Just daily functioning in our marriage was overshadowed constantly by the awareness of the influence of the PTSD. For many years I worked at making it work. I journaled, got counseling, read everything I could get my hands on, joined the support group, took classes, etc. And it helped. It was intense and hard work. I am glad that he got help too and was willing to talk with me about stuff.

"But recently I have noticed that things are going better without all the conscious effort. All the work we put into understanding it and each other, and doing the things that were good for us and the relationship, are finally paying off. The intensity is lifted. The good things we put into place are starting to take hold without so much focused effort. I did not know it would get better.

"We are laughing more and discovering silly moments (we could have our own comedy show if rating was not an issue)! We are enjoying passion and sex (when things work) more than ever. We pray together, which is huge. It is so wonderful to be able to enjoy each other rather than analyzing all the time. I know the PTSD will always be there. And I keep on guard for triggers. But what a nice place to finally be in, where we can experience joy and love and peace for the first time in our lives.

"At our group support meetings, I notice those who have fulfilling (not perfect) marriages and relationships with their vets are those who have been at it for years. And are doing the right things. Those who struggle are mostly those who are new to PTSD. So be encouraged that the hard work will pay off. It does get better as long as we make good choices and he is willing to do his part too. Even if he is not, our good choices will pay off."

We and our vets wake up each day with new opportunities for growth. Faith and love are powerful in the successful process of growing with PTSD. Connection with God and connection with others who care are common threads woven into the lives of those who find fulfillment while living with PTSD.

We all would welcome the day a complete and total cure for PTSD were discovered. But until then, let us continue to support and LOVE OUR VETS. They deserve it!

$\mathscr{L}$♥

4. Can I help him?

Simply put, you can help him, but you cannot fix him. Curious how it seems that those of us who are drawn to vets are also very caring people. It would be an interesting study to follow the lives of those who fell in love with vets either with or without knowledge of their PTSD. I often wonder if there is something at the subconscious level that identifies the disorder and resonates with it. Maybe we are more of a match than we realize. Most of the people I have met who love their vets are by nature very loving and caring people, the type I would want around if I had a problem.

The drawback to being of that nature is that we are wired to care, as well as to fix the problem. It is in our nature to find the problem and solve it. How simple. But alas, here we are with a lifelong problem that does not have a fix. The good news is that it is not a black and white issue with only two extreme options. There is plenty of middle ground where we can indeed be of help. The key is to hold on to ourselves as we reach out. Do not kill yourself in trying to fix him. As we take care of ourselves and remain mindful of our own needs, we have more strength from which to draw. It is a balance. We have to stay nourished and nurtured ourselves on a continuous basis if we are to be able to give and encourage and help them.

It is very meaningful to our vets when they see us wanting to understand them. Anything we can do to learn more about PTSD and about them will help. Be willing to talk with them about it whenever they're open. It is also helpful to refer to the PTSD as "The PTSD," rather than just "PTSD." Somehow that label keeps it separate and objective rather than infused with him.

One of the things we can do is to love him physically. For wives, this is not just making love (which is really good too!), but it can be lots of hugs, and pats, and foot rubs, and hand squeezes, and kisses on the cheek, etc. You might run up to him (be careful not to alarm him) and say, "Oh, this came for you in the mail today." And then give him a big hug and slurpy kiss. Or, as you pass in the hallway, just grab him and squeeze him and say, "Have I told you today how much I love you?" Spontaneity and randomness are really fun! You will find a wellspring of love that you never knew you had. Funny how it is that when we give we also get a blessing ourselves!

Another way we can be helpful is in relation to anniversaries. Have you ever asked him about his anniversaries? These are the dates that were significant in his time of serving and very likely significant in his trauma. Ask him to share those times with you and anything about them that he feels comfortable sharing. Make notes of them for yourself. Then throughout the year, keep these in mind. It may be helpful to draw his attention to them when the time comes if you see him starting to have more severe problems; or it may just be helpful for you, as you remember these times are harder for him whether he is conscious of it or not. I have found that sometimes our vets are very keenly aware of these anniversaries; other times they are relieved to be reminded since that offers an explanation for their unusually acute difficulty. And a bit of hope that things will ease up a little after the date has passed.

Words of affection and affirmation are huge to them also. One of the drawbacks of PTSD is how it erodes one's self-esteem. Anything you can do to build him up is really important. Tell him how much you appreciate how he keeps the family safe. Or thank him for doing chores, or for hugging you when you need it, or paying bills, etc. Let him know how much you admire his tender heart or the kind words he said to someone. For some it may be a stretch, but getting into the habit will eventually begin to help him as well as you. We tend to get nitpicky and negative. That is just being human. If we can keep our sense of humor a little better and let go of the things that really don't matter, we'll feel much better.

Anna was feeling irritable around her husband's sixtieth birthday (maybe hormones, or lack of sleep, or not feeling loved, lack of chocolate, etc.). Whatever the reason, she was not really in the mood for a happy birthday. So she decided to try to come up with a homemade card, listing all the things she loves about him.

She thought it would be a good exercise but was kind of doubtful that she could do it. She sat down to write, hoping to come up with sixty things in a week's time. Twenty minutes later she had sixty and could not stop. Do you know how much she fell in love with him all over again that week? And when she gave him the card, his eyes welled up with tears. "No one has ever given me a card like that before. Thank you." They both were deeply touched. And he has that card to look at when he feels discouraged or depressed or unloved.

Be creative. Whether you're a parent, friend, spouse, or other loved one, the sky's the limit to your expression of affection for your vet. For instance, if you don't mind a little cleanup afterward, you might try what Bethany did. She noticed her vet was really down one morning, so she took advantage of the steamed-up bathroom mirror to do some artwork. She wrote something affectionately cute and drew something naughty. He loved it! Good thing the kids were gone.

Most vets feel unsafe. They long for someone they can trust. Anything you can do to help him feel safe is a huge help to him. One way I have seen is through listening. Really hear him. Encourage him to talk when he feels like it. To share his dreams or nightmares. To share his memories, whether pleasant or horrific. Do not interrupt. Do not judge. Any criticism will shut him down. One wife I knew was constantly putting down her man. He was really shut down. No way would he ever feel safe enough to open up to her. Another wife I knew was a non-stop talker. She, apparently, was incapable of listening. Words went just one way. Don't tell, but once when I was on the phone with her, she was just babbling on and on. I couldn't get a word in, or if I did, she just changed the subject back to herself. So I set the phone down, went and did something, then came back and picked it up. She was still talking. If I were her husband, I would want to live in my cave too.

Another way you can help him is to encourage him to get the help he needs. This can be tricky because you do not want to nag, just encourage. It may be going to a counselor, a VA support group, a Pointman group, AA, taking a walk, or reading something beneficial, etc. You cannot do this alone, and the more help he can surround himself with, the better for both of you. Ultimately it is his choice. Unless, please take note, unless he is abusing substances detrimentally and/or people are in danger. If he is in any way harming you or anyone else, then it is essential to have an intervention of some kind. The family and other loved ones need to rally around him in love, tough love, to ensure he receives the treatment he needs.

It may seem like an uphill battle, but be encouraged that your love and support can go further than you realize.

✍

5. What about his constant negativity? It really gets to me.

Understanding goes a long way toward helping one tolerate another's negative behavior. Why are our vets plagued with such negativity? Why are they prone to being skeptical and fearful and angry and irritable? Sometimes it helps to brush up a bit on our PTSD information. Then allow ourselves to journey back in our minds as if we were there with them in their trauma. Sit with it. Feel the terror. The aloneness. The dread. The shock! The stench of death.

That exercise can be painful and evoke a variety of feelings in us. But that is good every now and then in order to retain our compassion. And compassion is a companion to understanding.

It is also necessary for us to remind ourselves that we cannot fix them. It is not our job—even if it were possible. But we can help. Talking with them is good. Bringing their attention to the constant negativity can be an eye-opener to them. Often they are not even aware of their down-ward spiral. Asking questions is also good in that they help preempt defensiveness on their part.

Vickie and her husband had a routine of starting the day by dis-cussing all the things that were on the day's agenda. Without fail, every time, he ended up reciting all the things that could possibly go wrong. His mind was encumbered with visualizing every potential disastrous scenario. In contemplating his trip to the bank, he anxiously talked about dying in a car accident, having to wait in long, horrible lines, getting a new inexperienced teller who took forever, and then getting robbed on the way out to the car. (At that moment some of us might have been inclined to grab him and shake him and scream, "Snap out of it, Eeyore!")

Fortunately, Vickie's approach was much more effective. Calmly, with-out getting riled herself, she gently called it to his attention. "Are you aware that your thoughts are spiraling downward? Can we think about the good things in store today? And we have so much to be thankful for." She wrapped her arms around him and told him how much she loved him. "I know you have a hard time with anxiety, but sometimes I feel pulled down when you talk like that." She was able to draw his attention to it and at the same time express her feelings in the form of an "I" message.

Staying aware of our feelings is crucial to keeping ourselves from being consumed by negativity. We have the choice to be thankful and do things that are going to uplift us physically and emotionally.

Rachelle took a different approach. There were times when she felt like she was the recipient of a dump-truck load of garbage. Ken would rant and spew out all sorts of anger and frustration. Pure negativity. It was not always aimed at her, but she happened to be the nice person with a good heart who cared enough to listen. And take it. And take it some more. Over and over.

One day she realized it was not healthy for either of them. She did not like the way she herself was becoming negative. She felt the down-ward drag. And she often felt obligated to try to cheer him up at those times. If only she could say the right thing, perhaps she could fix him. Neither was a healthy response.

One thing they both enjoyed was a good sense of humor (which, by the way, often goes a long way in resolving conflict). So she shared with him that when he spouted off his garbage she felt like he was a dump truck. And she did not want him to do it anymore. Her tone of voice and caring heart were well received. He admitted that he did not like doing it. As a result, they agreed that when he started dumping, she would make the noise of a truck backing up: "Beep! Beep! Beep!" It worked. Now they can smile when he starts to dump. By the way, he got her a toy dump truck for Christmas.

Our vets will always struggle with the downward pull of impending doom. We cannot eradicate that. But we can come alongside them and love them in it. And we can provide so much encouragement to them by our positive outlook and our reminders of the many blessings we do have.

$\mathcal{L}$♥

6. Why am I sometimes overcome with this awful fear? How do I handle it?

All of us are fearful of something. Usually it is what we dread losing the most. For some it may be losing a child, our marriage, losing love, or losing the man we so deeply love. For others it may be loss of independence, health, freedom. And for all of us losing our life—or anything else that is precious to us.

Like pain, fear is our body trying to warn us. To inform us. To alert us of danger. And as difficult as it may be, we need to listen to it. Stop. Feel it. Tune in and try to understand what our inner self is needing.

Our vets are often plagued or consumed with fear themselves. As trauma survivors, they are still in survival mode. Much of that wears off on us, even if we do not realize it. So not only do we carry their fear, we compound it by adding our own.

The first step in handling our fear is to own it. Name it. Recognize it. And accept it. There is nothing inherently bad about being afraid. The danger comes either by ignoring and stuffing it, or by feeding it.

After we acknowledge our fear, then we need to think about it. Why am I afraid? Is it rational? Can I reason myself through this? Some have benefited from journaling and others by talking. Just like all our unwelcome feelings, we have the choice to process it in a healthy way—to find healthy outlets for it.

If there is something worthy of our attention, such as an abusive situation, then we need to immediately do something about that. If it is just a nebulous feeling hanging over us like a heavy fog, then we can explore it further. Good counselors are very helpful in aiding us as we dig down to the deeper layers and get to the stuff we can work with.

Talking with other vet wives and loved ones is truly a lifesaver. Brandi was in a new relationship with her vet. Although a bit uneasy, she went to meet with some other ladies who were also involved with PTSD vets. What a relief for her to hear that her fear was common.

"I just am overwhelmed at times with this awful fear. My stomach gets to churning and sometimes I just want to bail." The discussion centered around the fact that we never can be quite sure when our vets will react. And when they do, what the fallout will be. That is just something we learn to accept. As loved ones living with them, we are the first to get it. So it is understandable that we carry some level of fear. Our bodies are helping us stay alert and on guard.

But sometimes that is not good for us. So it is crucial that we learn to be aware of when our fear is consuming us and putting a barrier between us and our vet. "Perfect love casts out fear." On the flipside, fear casts out love. When I am fearful, I am focused on me. When I am loving, I am focused on someone else. Reaching out and caring will mysteriously dispel the fear.

In a nutshell, the best thing we can do with our fear is to protect ourselves from real danger, feel the feelings, process them in a healthy way, and love our vets.

7.   How can I get friends and family to understand?

You can't. Even with as much information as is available about PTSD, one really cannot know what it is like to live with it until they do it. One evening a new lady who had been a vet wife for more than thirty years came to our Love Our Vets support group for the first time. She just sat quietly observing as we all talked. No expression. Just listened. When it was her turn to share, she just burst out in tears. "You all know! You understand!" She sobbed with relief. "You really know what I've been going through!"

Our hearts went out to her as she tearfully told her story and how hard she had tried to get her grown children and her friends to understand. It was like she was dying alone in the desert, shriveled up from thirst. Along we came in our desert-ready tour bus with gallons and gallons of water and tons of love.

It does help to educate those around us who are significant in our lives. There are some good classes available through the VA and veterans' assistance centers. Some counseling facilities also offer classes and support groups. There are new resources popping up every day online. Books, groups, websites. Any information you can pass on is helpful.

But it is probably not possible or necessary that they totally get it. In one sense, it is a relief that maybe you can stop trying so hard. Also perhaps it will lighten your already overbearing load to have one less task to worry about. Ask yourself, Why do I want them to understand? Do I need sympathy? Do I need help? Do I need an excuse for something? Do I feel I have to defend him?

After thinking about it more, I have come to realize it is easiest to more or less just let it go where others are concerned. You and I can find the support and understanding we need from those who also live in our shoes. We find comfort and hope when we connect with others who know and feel and care. And we can offer mutual encouragement and practical help as we connect together.

When I do decide to offer some sort of "explanation" to others, the best way I have found to communicate it is with a nice short statement. And then leave it there. Something that will offer enough of an explanation to relieve myself and to help them. Then let it go. A few things you might consider using are as follows:

"Yeah, he really has a hard time being around people."

"It has not been a good day around here."

"The PTSD makes it hard for him to _____."

"His stress tank is full and there is no room for anything more. Anything stressful will put him over the top."

"It is a baffling and frustrating disorder."

"We have good days and bad days."

"He can't handle loud noises."

"He does better with_____"

"Thanks for caring."

In your mind and heart, bless them for caring and trying to understand, but give them grace that they will never experientially know what you are going through. And that is okay. It hurts. It feels lonely and scary. But it is okay.

8. **How do I keep from going crazy when he is triggered or deeply depressed, or his meds are not balanced, and he is not rational? I get so frustrated that I cannot communicate with him. I feel so helpless.**

Helplessness is a horrible feeling. When our vets shut themselves off from us and the rest of the world, we are left hanging. Almost like dangling from the edge of a cliff. Desperately trying to hold on. And often wondering why.

One thing I learned early on was to remember that it is not me. It was the seasoned ladies who have been doing this for decades who helped me gain that insight. It is not you. It is not us. There is not some magic thing we should be doing to fix them.

In order to keep from going crazy, we also need to learn to take care of ourselves and let him be him. I can care without losing myself and my healthiness. Sometimes in trying desperately to fix him when he is in a bad mood or in pain, we offer up ourselves as a sacrifice in exchange for a solution.

Also, we need to embrace joy more. It is so easy to just let the heavy stuff pile up on top of us. But we can break through it! As Geri Ann shared, for her it was remembering to look up through the piles at God. That step of faith gives her the boost she needs. And perspective. "I am a fun person! I want to laugh more. And enjoy him more. And enjoy me more!" Today can be a good start.

A few more general insights from those who have successfully loved their vets are spelled out below:

- Communicate clearly; be sure I have heard him correctly and be sure he hears me. Make sure he hears me correctly. Sometimes he can distort what he hears.
- Always ask for what I need.
- It is okay…necessary…for me to tell him when I need to that I do not like what he is doing. And it is okay for me to feel afraid at first.
- Do not own his anger and behavior. Be like a reflector shield. I do not need to be embarrassed by his outbursts…they are his.
- Take time to get alone to my special place. Take care of me.
- Marriage will have ups and downs; that is normal.
- All relationships have their ups and downs.
- Be gracious when he is forgetful.
- Remember that my nonverbal communication is very important. Show my love; don't just say it.
- Many of them are afraid we will abandon them. Reassure them that we are not going anywhere and that it is okay for them to disagree with us. We are here. We love them.

ℒ❤

9. When does my compassion and big heart help, and when does it do damage?

The key is boundaries. Healthy boundaries. If we let his problems rob us of our health, then our compassion is no longer good. If we let our compassion enable poor behavior on his part, then it is no longer good. Too many well-meaning wives and loved ones have done harm unintentionally. We want to help and we care deeply. But there is a point at which compassion is needed and a point at which it is deceptively motivating.

Nona's husband was severely affected by PTSD. She had such a big heart that her whole life centered around him. Sadly, in that process she neglected her own heath, in spite of the fact that she was aware of a serious health problem. She ended up becoming disabled herself because she allowed her misguided compassion to overrule her wisdom.

Eva's vet took advantage of her compassion by running her ragged and by using his PTSD as an excuse for other bad behavior. She was under the mistaken notion that she would be a bad person if she did not always cater to him. On the contrary, when she finally discovered the concept of healthy boundaries, things actually got better for both of them (not right away, but over time).

Compassion is a treasure. When wisely used, it is a life-giver. Both to the compassionate person and the receiver of it. As hard as it may be, it is good for us to periodically read about their war experience. Or listen as they talk. We have to allow ourselves to become vulnerable enough to feel the moment as if we were there. That will go a long way in realigning our perspective and understanding their unending struggle for survival. It also helps us "differentiate" by remembering that it is his trauma. And it keeps his troubles from becoming ours.

Then we need to be free to express our compassion. Frequently. Nellie shared this tender moment:

"One night, after a bad day, I was cuddling in bed with Jared. He commented that he was not feeling good. He said he was feeling 'strange and weird.' My first thought was to jump right in and fix the problem for him. To get him out of weird as soon as possible. But instead I just laid there and listened. I continued to hold him as he held me. I gently asked him to tell me more. He was quiet. I then asked how feeling strange was different from feeling tired. My tone of voice was truly interested and caring. I know he sensed that it was probably safe for him to open up. He couldn't specify but just said, 'It's in my head…I'm just a head case.' Then I wrapped my arms around his head and gently pulled him to my chest. I held him compassionately and said, 'I love your head. Just the way you are. I love *you*.' All was quiet as I felt him relax. He rested and we held each other. Then we began just talking, opening up, and sharing things with each other. The next morning he was much better. And we went deeper in our relationship than ever before."

Nellie learned a valuable lesson that night. *Do not try to fix*…just love. *Be with*. Fixing says, "You are not okay until you are better…you have to change to be good enough." We are not told to fix each other's problems, but to bear each other's burdens. That is compassion. That compassion heals. Scientists and psychologists are discovering that healing the actual physical brain happens with love and "being with." The body chemistry changes when it is being loved.

Connection is the key.

Suffering will happen, and it is not the worst thing. Suffering alone is the worst thing. God never intended us to be alone. Compassion expressed by closeness and acceptance goes deeper and further than we can imagine. And we ourselves are also blessed as we give love.

$$\mathscr{L}\!\!\blacktriangledown$$

10. Is there a difference between the vets who discover their PTSD soon after the trauma as opposed to those who have gone decades without knowing what was wrong?

They are finding that the sooner someone with PTSD gets help, the better. The longer the trauma goes undiagnosed and unacknowledged, the more ingrained it becomes. Over time the brain becomes used to operating in emergency mode 24/7. The PTSD is still similar, but the treatment will be more effective the earlier it begins.

As wives and loved ones, our role is still the same, whether their trauma was two years ago or forty years ago. We love them, encourage them to get the help they need, maintain healthy boundaries for ourselves, and take care of our needs. There is always hope.

11. How do I know if this is normal relationship stuff or if it is PTSD stuff…and does it matter?

As we know, every relationship has challenges. That is just the reality of two human beings relating. As one minister put it, "The problem with marriage is that we marry a sinner." So in a way that is good news and kind of lifts the pressure we feel because we know there is just a certain amount of struggle and stuff that we should expect.

However, throw PTSD into the mix and the normal problems become turbo-charged. As wives and loved ones of veterans with PTSD, we have to adjust to a "new normal." Being aware of it is a good first step. Learning coping skills for ourselves is a good second step. Surrounding ourselves with a healthy support network is another helpful step. It is also crucial to encourage our vets to get the help they need.

Finally, a huge contributor to a successful and fulfilling relationship is to get counseling together. This helps in acquiring good communication patterns and other healthy ways to relate and grow together.

When we don't expect perfection and are willing to work with what we do have, we are more likely to see the good and to build on it.

12. I really want to make him happy. Things are so pleasant when he is. Why do I feel so frustrated and like a failure if he is not happy?

Where in the world did we get that mandate inside of us that we are responsible for making others happy? And why does it take most of our lives to figure out that not only do we not *have to*, we *can't*. It is not our job to keep anyone happy. Not our husband, our children, our boss, our friends, our coworkers, our parents, the mailman, strangers, or anyone. Even if it were our responsibility to keep everyone happy, it is not humanly possible. And in my experience, even God does not make it His aim to keep everyone happy. There must be something even better. Higher. More important than a temporary feeling.

But in the meantime, while we are living day to day with other people, it truly is nicer when we are all happy. And most of us would sacrifice in order to keep that pleasantness in our homes. The problem is that when we spend all of our good energy on an impossible task, we end up spent. Depleted. And ultimately no one is happy.

Felicia was on the verge of a major meltdown. How did she get to that point without realizing there was a problem? Like many of us, Felicia really loved her vet, Trent, and did all she could to show it. However, somewhere along the way, she forgot her own needs. In her case, due to a health issue, she was limited in spare energy for social occasions.

Sometimes as well meaning as he was, Trent would forget about her limitations and make plans for them without discussing it with her. This particular occasion was a late evening out for dinner and a show with friends. When he informed her of the plans, she wanted to implode. She panicked inside! At that moment, she saw two options: Either say okay and keep him happy at the expense of her health and pay for it all the next week, or say no for her health and risk his anger, which would backfire and make her lose more energy ultimately from the conflict.

The following is an excerpt from her journal as she worked through the dilemma:

"I am feeling tempted to abandon myself and my needs to keep him happy. Part of me is trying to be determined not to go because I know what it will do to me. I am afraid that I will crash and take a real setback, which I dread especially because I have been doing so much better lately. It really bothers me that he did not talk about it with me first. Ticks me off! We need to get better at deciding things together. Well, I will plan to stick up for myself graciously, but it feels very uncomfortable. Scary. But I promised my body I would start listening to it more and not subjecting it to suffering to keep others happy.

"I told him that I was sorry I could not join them tomorrow. Trent is not happy. At all. But I am taking care of myself and he is not happy about my boundaries. It is scary, but something inside me feels stronger. I know it is right, but doing this is new to me. Why do I feel I have to fight for it? But if I gave in I would be sicker. I would be so resentful, and they would not necessarily be any happier as a result.

"Felicia, be strong; be gracious. Love myself and nurture me and don't be afraid that they may not like it. Help me God to do the right thing and do it graciously.

"And what a free feeling to remember that he does not have to be happy all the time. How freeing!"

Felicia and Trent had a really good talk after all had settled down. She was able to share her needs and articulate them better. And he was able to talk about his perspective too. They are doing much better. And Felicia has been meltdown-free for a good while now.

Another loved one of a veteran with PTSD adopted this phrase somewhere along the way on her journey. She no longer feels obligated to run herself into the ground attempting to keep everyone happy. Most of us would also benefit from adopting it as our own. Her phrase is, "It's my turn!"

All the work we put in to trying to keep them happy can be more useful if we invest it in keeping ourselves healthy. Working hard to keep from setting them off will only distance us from them and burn us out. But when we focus on being ourselves and living life fully, then we are more fulfilled and the relationship can grow. And the more we are good to us, the better it is for them.

13. Why do I feel like a referee between him and other family members?

You feel like a referee because you're trying to be a peacekeeper. We know well that the peacemakers are blessed, but sometimes it feels a bit cursed. A referee's job is to remain neutral, constantly watch everyone, make judgment calls when there is a disagreement, enforce the penalties, and make everyone hate them. Often with very little pay.

Pause for a moment to think what you are trying to accomplish. How is it working out for you? Is it realistic? Are you paying too high a price for the results? If what you are doing results in everyone getting along and you and your vet are doing great, then you might as well keep it up. However, in most cases it just makes things worse.

If you're trying to protect a child from physical abuse, then acting as a referee is too mild a solution. More drastic measures need to be taken. Now! On the other hand, if your goal is to keep everyone happy, then you might as well put your feet up, put in your favorite chick flick and indulge in a box of chocolates. The outcome will be about the same. We cannot keep anyone happy, let alone everyone!

Marla was at her wit's end. She and her vet were raising two teenagers. Combine PTSD with raging adolescent hormones, throw in a few pre-menopausal symptoms, and there you have the perfect recipe for either total insanity or homicide. Minimally, a few doors slammed too hard and holes punched in the walls.

Marla spent most of her time at work checking her cell phone for messages from any of them. Braced for trouble at any moment. Sound like PTSD for her? And when they were all home together, there would usually be butting heads. By the time she took off her black-and-white striped shirt and her head hit the pillow, she crashed. Wondering if she could do it one more day. The irony is that all her efforts did not seem to fix things. Just perhaps provide a buffer at times. Would she be able to hold out for several more years? Perhaps…if they lived through it and the house was still standing.

As humorous as it can sound, truth is that it is sad. How she grieves that the people most precious to her cannot get along. And how utterly helpless she feels. Rightly so.

When we as caregivers and lovers of our vets feel helpless, there are two things we can always do. First, take care of me. What do I need? Then, do it. Now. Secondly, where can I get help? Marla had many options. Her connection to our Love Our Vets support network was a lifeline. Also, she found that the school counselor was a big help. She checked into other resources for all of them and also encouraged her husband to get the help he needed. Then they signed up for family counseling—all together in spite of the reluctant participants. But Marla's cleverness and love won out when she bribed them with their greatest weakness: her chocolate chip cookies.

Take it one day at a time. And never be afraid to ask Him for help.

14. How do I hold on to my individuality and not become fused with him and his PTSD?

There are a few things we can do to hold on to ourselves in a healthy way while living with the PTSD. First, acknowledge that he has it and it is his PTSD. Not mine. Together we deal with the PTSD, but it is his.

Secondly, be aware of what is going on inside of me. Tune in to physical and emotional signals that indicate that I am not grounded. Those signs vary. For some it is difficulty sleeping. For others it may be irritability, feelings of claustrophobia, or loss of freedom. Maybe it is digestive issues. Or headaches. Maybe it is unexplained weight gain. Or binge eating. It could be chewing fingernails, pulling on hair, or grinding teeth. We need to honor our inner wisdom, and pay attention when it cries out to us for help.

Thirdly, take time for you. The phrases, "It's my turn" and "It's my time" are beautiful. Appropriate for us in this phase of our lives. Whether twenty-six or sixty-six, we need to live. What are our dreams? Where are we utilizing our talents that we just love using? What do we do that brings us joy and replenishes our energy? Those are the things to weave into our lives.

When our entire existence centers around living for our vet, we wither. We grow numb. We shrivel up. And that is not life. Where did we get the notion that our vets want us to lose ourselves in caring for them? Most of our vets want us to be fulfilled. When we come home from an uplifting activity, they benefit. They want to see our joy. They are energized when we are too.

15. What is the importance of physical touch (sex, kissing, hugs, etc.)?

Simply put, it is huge! Vitally important. You may recall the studies years ago in which they discovered that infant orphans who were never cuddled died, and those who were thrived. We, as adults, are no different. As human beings, we have been designed to need each other. Physically and emotionally.

There is a whole new outpouring of neurological research. Studies of the brain reveal that actual physical healing occurs when two people are connected emotionally and physically. Chemical changes also occur immediately when two people hug or kiss. To say nothing of the closeness that takes place in sexual intimacy.

Unfortunately, some of the medications that our vets take have a negative impact on their sexual function. So in some cases intercourse is not an option. But there are many creative alternatives. Studies show that even just holding hands or cuddling increases the positive energy in our bodies and emotions. Also, do not pass up opportunities to have fun. Play together! Any closeness will bring you together. And the love and joy will continue to grow. Please do not pull away from him. He needs you more than you realize. And you need him!

Our vets have brains that need healing. Our loving touches throughout the day and night can get through to them more than any drug ever could. It is a mystery how our physical, mental, emotional, and spiritual components are so intertwined. Isn't it wonderful that we do not have to understand it all in order to benefit? It is really quite simple. Anyone can give a hug.

Our vets also have huge hearts, just like we do. And we all need to be loved. Whether married, lovers, siblings, children, relative, or friend, never underestimate the power and blessing of a simple loving touch!

$\mathcal{L}$

16. How do I help him find the best balance between veteran-related activities that may stir up the PTSD, and participating in them for the benefit of the camaraderie and positive aspects? When is it good and when is it not good?

As loved ones, we can be very helpful to our vets by offering them wisdom to consider. Things to think about. Questions that allow them to reflect. One drawback of PTSD is that it often interferes with normal thought processes. There seems to be a bypass, a sort of short-circuiting that occurs. That makes it difficult for them to perceive things accurately and also to derive wisdom from their own introspection. So as outside observers (who care!) we can assist them in their thought processes. We can offer our observations as well as questions to encourage them to draw from their own insight.

Alice got to the point that she dreaded the nights when Ralph would go to his Vietnam vet meetings. Although he said he enjoyed hanging out with the dudes, he would always be in a horrible mood when he got home—and for a few days following. Irritable, depressed, snappy, on edge. His sleep was also significantly disturbed.

Finally she decided to talk with him about it. (Why does it take us so long to communicate?) First she asked him how he felt about the group. His response was, "Oh I don't know." So she shared with him her observations of his behavior and told him she was concerned.

"Are there both good things and bad things about it?" she inquired further. "Do you think the guys and the conversation stir things up inside of you?"

Then he began to think as she continued to sit with him and hold his hand. Then more stuff came out. It was a really good time of opening up for both of them.

The fact that he was now able to reflect and observe himself was where he needed to start. And how important it was for Alice to stay with him in love and compassion and strength on her part. She helped him think through what he needed and wanted. She also reminded him that he has choices. He can choose to go or not, or just to go sometimes. But how great it was that he became aware (and will be in the future), which will empower him to make better choices for himself.

The challenge we all have is that life is never black and white. There seems to be some good and some bad in every decision. The more we and our vets can take the time to tap into our wisdom the better we will be able to make healthy choices. Talking things through and even praying together for that wisdom has proven to be a lifesaver for many.

$\mathscr{L}$❧

17. Is it possible to love someone when you do not feel loving or "in love"?

Absolutely! Or no one would ever get loved. Except in the movies. We grow up with that Cinderella fantasy, and most of us live our lives with that dream or expectation. We eat up romance novels and chick flicks. And we recall with fondness the thrill of our first "loves."

Now we are all grown up and the man we fell in love with has turned out to be a real human. Oddly enough so are we. And as long as we hold on to and perpetuate the fantasy that true love makes you feel giddy and have butterflies in your stomach, we will be miserable. And so will those around us.

Love is action. Not dependent on feeling. Often the good feelings follow the action, but not always. Love is doing something for the good of the other. Love is other-focused, not me-focused. That is the difference between a teenager and a mature wise adult. True love gives and cares and desires the very best for another. Anything less is not love.

The good news is that we do not have to wait to feel "in love" to love. When we do something kind for him, we will feel good just doing it. And so will he. Beverly's husband was a Vietnam vet. Rarely did our Vietnam veterans get a welcome when they came home. In fact, most of them were shunned and despised. After they had been married for awhile, Beverly felt the fires of passion dwindling. She did love him and wanted to feel it forever. But most of all she always wanted to show it in spite of her feelings, which come and go.

So one day she made a commitment to herself: "Every time he comes home from somewhere, I will meet him at the door and greet him as if he was just coming home from the war." Wow! The first time she threw her arms around him and kissed him passionately as if she thought he was never coming home. His response was bewilderment at first and then he caught the wave of passion. Then she looked him in the eyes and tearfully said, "Welcome home." They held each other as never before.

And ever since then that is their tradition. Beverly didn't wait to feel before she loved. Her love began as an action and turned into a feeling.

What does your vet need? What can you do today to help him in kindness? Perhaps you are a parent or other family member. The principle is still the same. You will probably not greet him passionately with lots of kisses at the door, but you can find ways to do loving things for him.

Whether or not we feel great about it at the time, love in action connects us with each other. And that connection brings healing and life to both people.

$\mathcal{L}$♥

18. **How do I encourage my vet to take care of himself (take meds, supplements, exercise, etc.) without being controlling or a nag?**

I think the key is the word "encourage." Encouragement springs from love. We truly want the very best for those we love. And we want them to stick around for as long as possible. Not only to just live, but to live well. When was the last time we expressed that love for our vets? Not in the context of wanting anything else. But just pure genuine care.

Additionally, it will do all of us good to keep in mind that they are adults and we can't control them. The more we remember that, the better the relationship, and the better we are as individuals. Too often the "encouragement" stemming from good intentions is perceived as nagging. Not good. Nagging tends to drive a person in the opposite direction. It also erodes the relationship. All of our communication should be drenched in respect. When our vets know that we respect them rather than trying to dominate and control them, they will be much more receptive—as any of us would be.

We who are givers by nature can burden ourselves with the false assumption that their health and well-being is our responsibility. This mind-set will in time erode our health and well-being. We need to give ourselves permission to let go and let them be the keeper of their own health. That freedom is a good thing for both of us, whether or not we agree with their choices. At times that is so hard! It eats away at us to see our diabetics chow down on ice cream and candy bars and not monitor their insulin. We cringe when we hear our vet say he is sick of taking pills and does not want to take any ever again.

Rather than just sit by and watch in fear, there are a few things we can do. First is to be aware of our feelings. For most of us it is an underlying fear of losing them. Fear of watching them deteriorate and be in pain. We experience anger and frustration too. Our job—for our benefit and theirs—is to take care of us. The better we are, the better chance they have.

We can also live what we "preach." Not only for our good, but perhaps our example can influence them in a positive way. As they observe our healthy choices and our living well, they will be more motivated to do the same. We can hope.

Another option is to invite them to join us. One vet wife and her husband both had health issues. Both struggled with weight, blood sugar, and other complications. Rather than just nag at him, she took the initiative to start walking. One day she invited him to go with her. Over time, they have developed a routine of going for walks together. And they love it!

We can also inquire. "What can I do to be most helpful?" Missy's vet hated taking all his meds and supplements, and he was very vocal about it. He was overwhelmed with the huge pile of pills and menagerie of pill bottles in the cupboard. "These nasty green and white pills, and spotted pills, and these giant horse pills, and this glop I have to drink…I can't take it anymore!!" After he calmed down a bit they had an actual conversation. Missy kept her head and remembered that this truly was overwhelming for him. And a hassle.

So, after talking about it, they agreed together that she would sort them out and put them in little plastic bags for each day. It has worked pretty well. She does not nag. And he does not have to be overwhelmed with the task of sorting them out. All he has to do is take them. She also has lightened up a bit and does not fall apart if he goes a day or two without. Missy realized that her encouragement was most effective when he remained in control. The key was for them to talk about it and together to arrive at a workable solution.

Another thing we can do it focus on the positive. They say that it takes ten positive comments to balance out one negative. Have we counted lately? It is really good to be there to encourage when they do take good care of themselves. No matter how little it may be, let them know how much you appreciate it when they take good care of themselves! And let them know that you know that it is not always fun, but you admire the times they take the steps to be good to themselves. Ultimately, because you love him and want him around as long as possible. And you want him to feel good. It also never hurts to remind him of how much better he feels when he is doing the best for himself.

When all is said and done (which it never is, but that is a fun phrase) know that we must be okay even if he doesn't take care of himself. We go on and make healthy choices for ourselves and continue to live our lives the best we can.

℘

19. As parents of a veteran, how do we know what our place to do is and when to just back off?

As parents of any adult child, it is a struggle to define our role. With the PTSD afflicting our child, it complicates things even further. All of the same principles that apply to wives and other loved ones apply to parents too. We cannot fix them. We have to maintain healthy boundaries. And often we may need to use "tough love" if there is substance abuse. Ultimately, we as parents still desire the very best for our child, whatever that may be. We have to leave ourselves and our interfering feelings out of that equation.

When parents have a decision to make regarding their vet, they need to stop and ask, "What is best for him? What is in his best interest? Where can he get the help and support he needs?" The hardest part is waiting and watching on the sidelines if he does not choose to get help, or if he continues destructive behavior.

Always treat him with respect. Be willing to listen when he needs to talk. Be willing to not probe if he does not want to talk. There is a fine line between respecting his privacy and encouraging him to open up. Again, be conscious to keep his needs at the forefront, not our feelings. It may feel hurtful if they do not choose to confide in us. It is not uncommon for vets to only feel safe with others who share their experiences. It is not personal. You are still and always will be Mom or Dad.

Life will be different from now on. As parents we need to let go of any former dreams we had for them and accept them as they are now. We may even grieve as we cherish the precious memories of cradling them in our arms. But now we must look ahead and encourage them to go forward with their life, which is still brimming with possibilities.

It is also helpful to acknowledge that they may not feel comfortable at family gatherings. Always allow them their privacy and freedom to refrain from participating if they need to be alone. But encourage them if you see them hiding in reclusion.

As far as advice, we know that questions and personal "I" messages carry a lot more weight than suggestions or orders (not a good idea for any PTSD vet!).

These parents of a veteran share the following tips:

- Read and learn all you can about PTSD.
- A strong relationship with God is paramount. For those that don't have that, it will be even more difficult to navigate these troubled waters.
- Although the waters might be smooth now, another storm could happen at any moment. Be prepared for unpredictable ups and downs.
- Don't let our parental emotions inhibit our objectivity as we assume the role of coach. We can't afford to take his behavior personally. Remember it is the PTSD, not us.
- Accept the fact that things will never be the way they used to be.
- Remember unconditional love.
- Resist the urge to offer quick fixes.
- Recognize that you might never know the details of his experience and it is okay if it is left unsaid.
- Encourage him (and his wife) to join a support group of positive people that would not dwell on the history, but be forward-thinking and accept what happened as providence.
- Do anything you can to help their children understand that at times daddy isn't doing well today and not feel like they are the issue.
- Express the pride that you have in your vet both verbally and physically. For men especially, don't hold back emotions and how you feel about him.
- Practice healthy boundaries. Often they can take advantage of parents. Remember the big picture. What is in his best interest and the interest of the children? Do not enable him in unhealthy ways.
- Keep life simple and understand when he declines invitations to events and gatherings.

- It is important to keep our spiritual life strong and our marriage strong in order to deal with the roller coaster ride!
- Always be available to listen (even if it is midnight).
- Finally, love them and grow with them.

✐♥

20. How do I remember that he is not the enemy?

Compassion. When we start to engage in a conflict, and feel that chill of anger starting to sizzle inside, stop! The last thing either of us needs is to attack each other. We both so desperately need each other! The irony is that the solution for our pain, fear, and rage is the very thing we are destroying. Closeness with each other. Connection.

Easy to say, I know. But consider what would happen if at that moment you ran into his arms and the two of you embraced. Silently. Just holding each other.

Sorry if I sound too idealistic, but don't mock it until you try it. There is something unexplainable about close, quiet contact between two people. It melts. It soothes. It calms. And even scientifically, it can change the chemical composition of our brains. The serotonin that the pharmaceutical companies are making billions on is right there for us. Anytime.

Compassion shifts our focus off ourselves and onto the wounds of another. It allows us to step back for a moment and see the situation in a whole different light. That person is hurting. This attack is really not about me. Or us. No relationship ever got better because of a fight.

We are not each other's enemy. We grow close and strong by uniting against the forces that attack and undermine and erode the closeness we have worked so hard to enjoy. And although it may be just one person who stops the battle, that is all it takes.

Compassion is what we need to hold onto as we love our vets.

Lily and Hal were having a rough day. It seemed as though they were at each other constantly. It was the night before Memorial Day. And Lily had forgotten the power of anniversary triggers. Until now.

That night in bed, she felt distant from him, but decided to try to let her guard down and come closer to him. She put her arm around him and just held him. Minutes later, he started to cry.

"I keep seeing dead people," he sobbed. She held him tight and wept with him. She just continued to hold him. She gently let him know he could share anything with her. That she was there with him. And for him. Together they would beat the enemy.

That night was the most precious time they had ever had. The comfort and intimacy they shared as they united against the trauma powerfully brought them close. "No one has ever wanted to listen to me before," he shared tenderly. And she thanked him for trusting her enough to open up and become vulnerable. She told him that made her feel so much closer to him.

Hold on to the vision of two together. Closeness is the strongest defense. The triumph of a successful day is well worth the effort.

$\mathcal{L}$❤

21. Why is he unable to handle conflict like "normal" couples? Just what are the rules for conflict when PTSD is a factor?

Most couples argue. All couples have disagreements. However, things are very different for those of us who have vets with PTSD. Nancy spoke for many of us when she expressed her frustration.

"Why can't I 'fight' or argue with him like most couples do and work through it? The rules seem to be different with him. I am afraid to be totally honest with him for fear that he will take it wrong or react. So how do I handle misunderstandings, miscommunications, differences of opinion, etc. if I cannot be totally honest and free to talk openly about my thoughts and feelings? I feel so stifled. I try to keep him from being triggered. And how do I keep myself from being triggered? It seems so unfair. I want to be able to fully express myself."

For such an emotional issue, I believe the answer lies in our left brain. We have to let go of relying on our feelings for sound behavior. Logically speaking, it is as if there are new rules. We have to abandon the assumptions we have operated on previously and create for ourselves a new system. The new rules are just for us. And although we feel helpless that we cannot alter these "rules," we do have the power to make choices. That is where our encouragement and hope come from. And ultimately everything good that we do for ourselves will benefit him and the relationship.

Let's look at this collection of new "rules," or guidelines to consider:

- It takes two to fight.
- I am responsible for my words and actions.
- I am not responsible for his responses.
- I have the freedom to express my thoughts, opinions, and feelings.
- Things go better if I can take time to process my thoughts and feelings before expressing them.
- I have the right to be safe.
- PTSD cannot think rationally when it is triggered.
- He will calm down.
- The best communication happens when neither of is aroused.
- There are many ways for me to express my feelings. I have options, and it is best to choose the healthiest.
- He will be most receptive to me when he is feeling safe.
- The first sentence out of my mouth determines whether or not he will be able to hear the rest.
- I need to be aware of my own feelings, especially what is going on in my body.
- It can be helpful for me to ask myself, "What do I need? Am I hungry? Tired? Hormonal?"
- I need to take care of my needs.
- I am free to let him know where I'm coming from and how I'm feeling in the form of an "I" message. Not an attack. Just a statement.

"Ouch! Honey, what is going on?" Or, "I am starting to feel anxious. Can we talk calmly?"

- I will not allow him to physically or verbally abuse me.
- It can be helpful for me to function like a mirror in helping him be aware of his actions. "You are really angry right now." Or, "Please do not raise your voice to me like that." Or if it is severe, "It is not okay to talk to me like that."
- Remember compassion. The trauma our vets lived through has made them unable to handle conflict without switching into survival mode, or take orders (that was what got them killed), or suggestions that come across as orders.
- Use questions in communicating. Ask rather than tell. Questions encourage communication and imply respect.
- Stay strong without getting angry. Anger loses power. The one who is not angry is in control.
- Always treat him with respect.
- It is my responsibility to not let things build up inside. I need to speak before I boil over.
- Remember the mental file folder. I do not have to speak right now. Nothing is urgent. I have the freedom to file it away and think about it more. Most likely the outcome and perspective will be better after a little time and introspection.
- Think ahead ten years. Will this issue matter? Will my behavior matter?
- When discussing behavior, be specific. Use examples that you both recall.
- Always let him know what you do appreciate about him and his actions. Be specific.
- The more I calm myself, the easier it will be for him to calm down also.
- After the storm is over, on another day, sit down and talk about it. What did I do that I want to do differently the next time? What can we both learn?

There are no winners in war. Not overseas or at home. Let's use our wisdom and grace to keep ourselves healthy and alive and to have a peaceful home.

$\mathscr{C}$

22. What can our family do when he gets so paranoid about crowds?

One of the classic symptoms of PTSD is intense anxiety around other people, especially crowds and public places. If they manage to brave the situation, they are functioning on high alert. Supervigilant. Consciously or not, many will position themselves in a spot where they can see everyone. If no one is there to "watch their back," they are compelled to not let themselves become vulnerable.

This can put a real damper on normal family living, activities, and outings. Tracy was describing their recent family trip to the large warehouse grocery outlet.

Mobs...crowds...lines...commotion. Not a good place for our vets. Her lament was that she had forgotten about his inability to function well in such a setting. Mildly put, it turned out to be a not very good shopping trip. So, do we not go shopping? Do we avoid fun events? If we do want to go somewhere, are we confined to always going alone?

The important thing we need to remember is to acknowledge their limitations and do what we can to be helpful. At the same time, we go on living. We do what we need to do. And it is good for our children to learn this too. Even if our vet's behavior is embarrassing at times, never ever treat him disrespectfully. Honor him and his war wounds.

However, a few things may help. First, talk about it with him. Do this before he finds himself in a situation where he feels cornered.

Ask questions. What does he need? What does he fear? Are there options? Can you all go at a time when there are fewer people? Is there another place that makes him feel safer? When you dine out, can you reserve the table in the corner? At church, is there a back row seat that feels more comfortable to him? (A few vets got together and were discussing the possibility of starting a church just for veterans. They ended up smiling as they envisioned no rows, just one gigantic circle of seats against the walls!)

The more we are conscious and respectful of them and their needs, while at the same time taking care of ours, the better we will all be.

23. Why is he so affected by the weather? How do I keep myself from being negatively affected too?

Weather impacts all of us, and particularly those who have been traumatized. Even though the weather itself may not have directly caused the trauma, the memories associated with that time and event can still trigger our vets. Often these triggers will occur subconsciously, unbeknownst to the person or their loved ones. For Aaron, an Iraq vet, it was the hot dry days that got to him the most. Whereas for Thomas, it was the humidity that hijacked him back to the jungles of Vietnam.

Another weather-related disturbance, known as seasonal affective disorder (SAD), also affects our vets. And although it can impact a lot of people, it brings down our veterans much more than the general population. The impending long cold winters and the dark rainy days really pull them down. Physiologically, our brains thrive on the vitamin D that comes from sunlight. Most of us do very well during the summer months. As fall approaches, we see our vets start to sink into depression, and increasingly more as the days get shorter and darker. And along with that, the lack of sunlight results in a loss of melatonin, which is our natural sleep hormone. So add to the mix lack of sleep and you get a pretty toxic combination. (One vet calls it a "warmed over dung day.")

Emily dreaded getting up each day because she would be greeted by her vet bemoaning the bad day ahead because it was raining. She found herself anxiously praying for good weather just to avoid the gloomy days inside her home. She also realized that she herself was starting to fight winter depression for the first time.

So she decided to talk about it with her husband Keith. She shared her feelings and anxieties and then asked him how he was feeling. For the first time he told her that the cold weather scares him. It frightens him. Not only does it weigh him down, he perceives it as a life threat. Cold weather meant some would not survive. And for other vets, the opposite would be true for severe heat.

As seasons change and the darker days approach, many find help from the full or broad-spectrum light boxes. They are available through the VA or various sites online. Just a short time each morning with the light on seems to provide a sort of simulated sunlight. Not only does this increase vitamin D production, but it also increases serotonin (happy hormone) and melatonin for better sleep. Be careful to use it only in the morning, or the body will get its sleep cycles all fouled up.

On a lighter note, one Vietnam vet wife (wishing to remain anonymous) shared this: Years ago, her vet lay in the jungle day and night cursing the endless tormenting rain. In his anger, he consoled himself by making a vow: "When I get home, whenever it rains, I am going to have sex!" Forty years later, he still is enjoying that vow. And so is his wife. (She is the one praying for rain.)

The bottom line is for all of us to be aware of how the weather affects us. Sometimes just awareness itself can be helpful.

24. Why should I pray for him?

Prayer is another way we can help them. In our "politically correct" (religious-phobic) times, people may shy away from talking about prayer or they may choose to redefine it. But most consider it in the traditional way to mean talking to God.

Praying for others is hard. It takes time and energy. But there are good reasons to make this investment. You may have discovered this already, but one benefit of prayer for others is that it actually helps us too. Ever notice that after praying for someone your attitude toward them has changed for the better? Maybe more compassion? Or perhaps patience. Or a new perspective?

And ultimately prayer helps the other person. I cannot explain why. I just know I have seen it over and over. Also, it's interesting to note that many studies done by non-religious medical professionals attest to the fact that prayer does make a difference. This is one of those mystifying things we just cannot explain.

✿

25. What should I pray for him?

There are no magic words. No right or wrong here. God is not interested in formulas or particular words. Just your heart. What does your heart desire for him? Pour it out. What does he need? Simply ask.

✿

26. What should I pray for me?

What do you need? Physically, emotionally, spiritually? Take time to be still. This can seem so foreign to those of us who are always on the go. And sometimes we find ourselves just staying busy in order to not feel. But it is time to listen to you. What is your inner heart crying out for? What is that ache inside of you?

Those of us who live close to our vets day after day can easily become so focused on them and their needs that we lose sight of ourselves. Or we may feel guilty even thinking of ourselves, as if that were selfish. "Always put the other person first," we have learned. Or is it okay to think about my needs now? Yes! If we don't take care of ourselves, we will burn out. We will shrivel up. Not much life left for me, let alone to give to others in need.

Talk honestly to God about anything and everything. Sometimes you may even not have words. Just weeping. Or sitting. Or walking. Or lying in bed in the middle of the night. It is so good to know we are heard. And loved.

≈•

27. He seems like he is always afraid. So anxious and fearful. How do I keep from getting paranoid myself, and is there a way I can help him be more rational?

As you know, PTSD means they were severely traumatized at least once and maybe many times, and most over an extended period of time. So the reality of danger was very real at one time. However, the traumatized brain still is programmed to operate in survival mode as if there could be an attack at any moment. So they do perceive threats that we do not.

One vet was terrified that someone would drive by and shoot them in their living room. He insisted that the sofa never be in front of the window. His wife thought that was ridiculous, but complied with the request.

Another vet braces all the doors in the house every night, has a gun in every room, and is fearful that at any moment someone might break in and sneak up on him while he sleeps. Another vet checks every nook and cranny in the house, including closets and cupboards.

Yet another vet is afraid every time his wife leaves the house that she will never come home alive. Others do all they can to prepare for impending disasters. Many operate under constant suspicion of conspiracies. One vet reacted in fear and rage while watching a movie that triggered something in him. He behaved just as if the people in the movie were out to get him. Another vet hit the floor in the movie theater when the actor began shooting.

These are very conscious fears in the forefront of their minds most of the time. Extremely real. We cannot change them. It is not something where we can just say the magic words and all will be fine. Normal. Peaceful.

But there are some things we can do. First, never belittle them. Whenever they open up to us, be there to wrap your arms around them and love them. They so need our comfort and understanding—even if we cannot really understand. It is also helpful to use these moments as a time to encourage them to open up more. Draw them out as you ask them to tell you more about how that feels. Just be there to listen and love, not judge or fix. And never, never (did I mention never?) laugh at them. Any form of ridicule will shut them down...perhaps indefinitely.

We can be a reflection to them to help them see their fears and anxieties. Often they are so immersed in their fears that they are unaware how debilitating they have become. A first step for them in dealing with the irrational fears is to be aware of them. We can lovingly help with that.

Another part of this is us. How do we keep their fears from becoming ours? Many of us have noticed ourselves beginning to do a perimeter check at night, and even throughout the day. Or, at the opposite extreme, we might wonder if we are being too cavalier when we don't worry about these things. We might second-guess our own rationality and wonder if we should start being more afraid.

It seems that the healthiest response is to stay connected to our inner wisdom. Recognize that his fear is *his* fear. Keep his feelings separate from ours. Also, we can use our brains and be alert for danger. Most of us are capable of staying safe. Neither should we allow ourselves to panic, or ruin our lives, by fueling the fear.

Somewhere in the middle is probably the peaceful and wise place. There is nothing wrong with letting him feel as safe as he can. I totally support that without feeling it. And I do appreciate that about him. A real plus is that I definitely feel safe around him!

One more thing to consider is praying together. I have seen couples who can pray about things such as safety issues and they do very well. One couple has a routine of always praying before they go anywhere. They also pray together every night before they go to sleep. He always prays for safety and protection. Not only does it bring them together, but they would testify that it really works.

Let us remember that his fear stems from his trauma. It is his trauma, not ours. That will help us differentiate and not carry it on ourselves. It also supports our understanding and compassion. I cannot fix it, but I can take care of me, and I can be a reflection when I need to be.

⌇❧

28. How much do we tell our kids and what do we say to help them?

A good question to start with is what is in their best interest? How will knowing be helpful to them? A lot will depend on their age and your individual situation. If they are teens or older, it would be beneficial to give them some pertinent material to read. This could be books, pamphlets, or info online (probably their choice). Many new websites are emerging every day to offer help for PTSD family support (see www.loveourvets.org for links). Additionally, more family classes are becoming available through the VA and other organizations. It might be worth your while to look into that.

Then sit down and have a family talk. Of utmost importance is their respect for him. The PTSD in no way should provide an excuse for disrespect. The bottom line is that Dad is a warrior. We are so grateful to him and proud of him. He was wounded as a soldier protecting his country. Even though we may not be able to actually see that wound, it is there deep inside him. It is sad that because of his experience in battle the war will always continue inside of him at some level.

This may be a very precious time of healing for all of you. Most likely there will be tears and hugs. All good. All necessary.

The ultimate purpose of informing them is to help them. The more they can understand and have compassion, the better it will be. You can describe some of the symptoms of PTSD so when the time comes they can say, "Oh, that's what that is." It is helpful to be able to refer to the PTSD as "The PTSD." Then talk with them about how they can best respond. Many of the same things we are focusing on will be important for them to learn also. How to speak respectfully but also get out if endangered. If Dad gets really angry, they need to know what to do. A plan. Who to call, where to go.

As humans and especially as children, when a parent is having a bad day we tend to assume it is our fault. Help the kids know that Dad will have hard days, and it is not their fault. It has nothing to do with them. He still loves them to pieces, and there is nothing they can do. Just love him and be on their usual best behavior.

They also will benefit from learning how to recognize and process their own feelings in a healthy way. They will experience fear, anger, frustration, and a whole lot more. It will be so important for them to learn early on how to work through their feelings in a healthy way. You might encourage journaling, or talking with you, or a counselor, or a close family friend.

The PTSD is our challenge as a family. We face it together. As we unite in loving support of our vet, we can become victorious one day at a time.

$$\mathscr{L}\!\!\!\!\bullet$$

29. What can I do about his anger and rage?

First and foremost, protect yourself and your children. Always. Your safety is top priority. If he is endangering you, get out. Now. Get help. If the danger is not immediate, it is wise to have a plan in place for if you do need to get out. Talk with other vet loved ones, the YWCA, women's crisis line, battered women's shelter, or other nearby social services.

Or perhaps his anger is not dangerous but disturbing. Karen put it this way: "He has too much anger, and it is oozing out all over me." She too was desperate to know what she could do to help. Another wife heard her vet say the other day in passing, "Sometimes I just feel like blowing something up!"

Remembering that we cannot fix them, there still are a couple of things that come to mind that we *can* do. First, help him be aware of his behavior. It is baffling that when they get triggered, they often are not consciously aware of how they come across. They may even deny it. Find a way to be a mirror to him. Gently. No anger on your part. Non-emotionally. Try asking or telling so he has an understanding of how you see him right at that moment. "You seem really angry right now." Or, "Is something triggering you?" Or, "You are really ticked off, aren't you?" If you can get him to be aware of his feelings and behavior and then to talk about it on a non-angry level, that is a great start.

We are not responsible for what we cannot control. Wonderful! Yippee! Remember that.

"WE ARE NOT RESPONSIBLE FOR WHAT WE CANNOT CONTROL."

But we can offer love and concern and constructive comments. What he does with them is his choice. But at least we know we have offered help. We have reached out.

Bumping it up a level, we can tell them that we do not like it. "You seem really angry right now. I do not like it when you talk to me like that." Or, "It scares me when you throw things." Or, "I don't like it when you yell." Or, "I do not like it when you_____." Be specific in identifying the action. If you are vague it is not helpful to him. He needs to know specifically what behavior is not acceptable.

Then leave the room. Or the car. Maggie shared with us that her vet would get triggered in traffic. One day she told him, "If you yell at me in the car, I am going to get out." Sure enough, she made sure she had money for the bus, waited for the next red light, and got out. He was pretty ticked off when she came home, but he has not yelled at her in the car since then.

One more thing that you can do is to encourage him to take an anger management class. His counselor should be able to get you information about those, or check online. Those are most beneficial when the individual is first aware of the problem and then aware of how it is hurting you. Their rage is often beyond their control, and in their deepest heart, they shudder at the thought of hurting you. So helping them get help is one of the best things you can do.

30. How do I accept him when at times I don't even like him?

Believe it or not, it is possible to accept a person while at the same time not like them. Or not approve of their actions. We know how important it is to accept and affirm our vets. All human beings thrive on acceptance, particularly those with trauma.

When something bugs us, we tend to pull away in judgment. "I'll treat him better when he deserves it, but not until then." That mind-set only hurts us and hurts them. Putting up walls never helps anyone.

Why do we have such lofty standards for others, but expect *them* to give us grace? Welcome to being human. I'm finding that the more grace I extend to others, particularly those who are irritating or disappointing, the more free I feel inside. Weird, huh? There is something about requiring others to be perfect that drains me of my good energy. When I can let go, and let them just be them, I am so much happier. You mean I do not have to control them? Kind of a nice concept. We are not responsible for anyone else but ourselves. That freedom allows us to accept them because there is nothing I must do to change them. Don't have to like it all, just realize it's a package deal. We people come in a premixed package.

So acceptance begins and ends with us. We get to learn not to impose our standards on him. Just take care of us. Unless it is a matter of safety or health. Then we need to work together on those issues. Acceptance does not rule out healthy boundaries.

Loving them without trying to change them is our aim. Albeit a life-long aim. Remember that our precious vets, as frustrating as they can be at times, are wounded warriors.

Valerie was having a hard time, wondering how she could muster up some good feelings toward Greg. She realized that a lot depended on her perspective. She put it this way: "I married him knowing he was wounded and handicapped. It makes it harder because the handicap is invisible. If I could see him with no arms or legs, it might make it easier to remember his condition."

Acceptance often begins with an action rather than a feeling. Love is action. Valerie stepped out in faith and began a hugging campaign. And then added a few kisses. And a few kind words. A few weeks later she realized it was coming naturally. She also said that it seemed as though Greg had changed. Hmm…wonder if he did, or does it matter?

Keisha struggled with feelings that came and went. Mostly went. Her insight was very valuable: "Sometimes I don't feel like I 'like' him because of how he acts. But I am also learning that I can still love him. Liking him is immature, and 'like' is self-serving…all about how it makes me feel. Love is mature. It is other-centered. And it is *soooo* much bigger than 'like.' I pray for God to enlarge my heart to love, selflessly, as He does. I want my love to engulf the 'like,' so that it doesn't affect my love when I'm not attracted to him at the moment."

One more thought: How much grace does he extend toward me? Am I always adorable? We need to remember to put the shoe on the other foot.

⌐♥

31. Why do I feel so angry and torn up inside when he walls me off and disconnects?

Being shut out from the one you love so much hurts like nothing else. It is like you don't exist. They cannot see you or hear you. They are not even there. It is frightening. And so terribly lonely.

Brittany noticed that Evan was sinking into another deep depression. Her stomach churned as she saw all the warning signs. He was pulling away. Shutting her out. When she looked into his eyes, it was as if he was not even there. Who knows when he would be "back." She felt like she was dying. Not even there. Sinking down herself.

That evening at her suggestion they went for a walk. As they walked, the painful silence hovered over them. Brittany was aware of her building anger. Resentment. Each time she tried to communicate with him, he just ignored her. He was with her physically, but the real Evan was hidden in his "cave." It hurt so bad. She felt the tingle of rage creeping up her spine and the stomach acid eating away at her. Suddenly, she burst out, "I can't take it anymore!" And she kicked a stone wall as hard as she could!

It wasn't until she was having a cast put on her foot that she was finally calmed down enough to think. What happened? How did she build up so much rage without realizing it, and then explode so violently that she broke her own foot?

Most of us have been there. Hopefully, we can become aware of our rage before it explodes. Our goal is not to not be angry, or not react, or not be affected by them, but to be aware of us. Be aware of what is going on inside of us. Learn to monitor our feelings. Tune in. What are our needs? What are we not getting that is making us so angry?

Brittany realized later that she was desperately needing him to connect with her. She needed him to hold her. To see her. To acknowledge her. To hear her. She felt like she was dying inside when she could not connect with him. Dead. Numb. Sinking. Hopeless.

We all must come to the point where we realize that we rely too much on our vet for our being. We have over the years made them our life. They are our existence. Intentions are good; result is not. When I depend solely on him for my fulfillment, I am not living. It's not fair to them nor to us to get our life from them. Our purpose. Our affirmation. Our self-esteem. No human being can give us all of that. No human being can meet all of our needs. We must learn to find our life from God and a relationship with Him. Only then can we be all He designed us to be!

When I choose to lean entirely on something or someone who is as unstable as a stack of blocks, I will fall when they do. But if I find my life and joy and purpose in something reliably solid, I can stand and live and thrive even when they tumble.

Brittany will always have her tender foot to remind her to stay centered, strong, and not rely on him for her well-being. Among the lessons she has learned is that when she is overcome by an urge to kick something, it is to her advantage to choose an object that will move. Additionally, she is becoming more in tune with her rising resentment and building anger. To feel the feelings. She is learning to discover her passions and talents and joys, and find fulfillment not only in the good days but in the cave days. She does not like it when he pulls away, but she is grounded now and learning that she can live her life just as fully no matter what his mood.

And it may sound crazy, but she swears that his cave days have been fewer and farther between.

32. Sometimes he gets upset by things people say or do and reacts in a way that really embarrasses me. What do I do?

This is typical for those with PTSD—and very frustrating for those who love them. Shelly was with her vet at church one day when someone was giving a testimony up front. Everyone else listening was loving it and getting good things out of it. The person sharing said something about her past that triggered Shelly's husband. Suddenly without warning, he stood up and said, "This is a bunch of #@! I'm not going to listen to this anymore." And out he stormed.

She was mortified—and at a loss for what to do. Where is the instruction manual when you need one!

Sometimes we feel obligated to defend them, and other times we're compelled to reason with them. Other times we just want to crawl under a rock or move to New Guinea.

Defending them is not our responsibility. It may make us feel a little better at the time, but is probably not a good idea. It's not up to us to explain everything to everybody. We just have to let some things go. And we cannot own their stuff. What they do is their responsibility. Yes, we may have to get splattered on occasionally, and pick up some messy pieces, but it's their stuff, not ours.

"WE CAN'T OWN THEIR STUFF."

Sometimes it helps to keep a sense of humor. Not sure exactly how that would look for Shelly, but it may be worth a try in other cases.

We might wonder if it's possible to reason with him and help him see that the "thing" was not really as bad as he perceived it. If that were to be effective, it would have to wait until later when he is no longer triggered. No sense trying to communicate rationally at the irrational moment of reaction. Trying later might be a good idea. Help him be aware of his behavior and how it was perceived by you. Share your "I" messages with truth and love.

And as a last resort, just give him space. And time to get over it. He will cool down eventually. We should be getting pretty good by now at giving him space. And that is a good thing for us too!

ℒ♥

33. How do I not let him rob my joy when we're with others and he's in a funk, or other embarrassing behavior?

It was Sandi's birthday and they all gathered downtown at her favorite fancy restaurant. Don was in a funk. She saw it coming but went ahead with the evening anyway, determined not to let his mood spoil her celebration. Just that effort to try to ignore him and pretend she was having a good time sapped her. She worked extra hard to keep everyone happy and tried to camouflage his irritability. He was rude to the server, complained about his food (actually not unusual), and wore an expression that screamed: "I am ticked off!"

The other family members and friends carried on as if nothing was wrong. But inside, Sandi was about to burst, either with tears or naughty words. (Looking back, she wished she had let a few choice words fly... just for fun.) But like us, she held it in. And her stomach started to hurt. Her head began to pound. Too bad she couldn't just chalk it up to old age!

Part of her wanted to issue a disclaimer to the others about his behavior. Part of her wanted to shake him and tell him to knock it off.

But the most painful part of her longed for him to just be nice, pleasant, courteous, and fun.

All of our emotions get stirred up when our vets go into their negative moods. We are learning that we can't change that. But we do have control over *our* responses. And we do have the right to speak up and voice our needs and desires. Sandi realized after the fact that it would have been better for her to have taken him aside and gently called his attention to his behavior. Sounds scary. Maybe evoke an eruption? Maybe make things a whole lot worse than they were? That is a chance we have to take—for our sake.

Sometimes when our vets are in a cave or get triggered, they're not aware of how they come across. Sometimes they are and it is deliberate. Either way, we can and should talk to them about it. Lovingly. Gently. Strongly. Calmly. "I noticed you are having a hard time tonight. Is there something I can help you with?" or, "You seem really upset about something. Are you okay?" Or, "Are you aware of how unpleasantly you have been talking and acting?" Or, "I know you are ticked off about stuff right now, but it would make me really happy if you could just be pleasant this evening just for me."

Later, hindsight led Sandi to realize she probably could have had that conversation before they left for the event. As soon as she knew he was having a bad time, she could have talked to him. Not only would that have helped him, but it also would have helped free her up from all that she was holding inside. Done respectfully, it could have gone something like this: "Don, you seem like something is bothering you." (Let him respond.) "Would you rather not go tonight? I can go alone if you're not up to it."

Show him that you recognize the pit he is in, and offer him the option of bailing out of the activity. You never know. Either he might have gladly stayed home, or else he might have picked up his mood. And if he insisted on going, at that point she could have requested that he try to be polite and pleasant.

We cannot let our fear of their response stop us from speaking up about what we need and want. They may not take it well, but that is not our responsibility. We are, however, responsible to speak up and voice our needs–if for nothing more than for us. To know we did what was good and healthy. And whether or not he changes at that moment, somewhere in his mind and heart it will register.

Keep in mind also that between episodes, when they are calm and the defenses are not up, that they are much more receptive to what we say. As long as we say it lovingly and calmly and in an "I" message form. Not accusatory or attacking but, "This is how I feel." "This is what I need." "I love it when you_____."

Bottom line, no one can take away your joy. It is *your joy*. If you have tried to communicate with him and he's still acting badly, then just let go. Can you picture him in another room? Focus on the love and fun and good things. Enjoy your friends and family. Soak it up. Just be you. Laugh. Live.

ℒ❧

34. What do I do with things that frustrate me but are not worth fighting over?

Welcome to life. Finally something that is fairly normal. All relationships have frustrations. Even healthy fulfilling relationships have to work through these things. But when you throw PTSD into the mix, the "rules" seem to change a bit. Anything we can do to defuse a situation before it gets ugly is best.

First, I never encourage anyone to fight. Fighting often does more harm than good. When two people escalate, emotions run wild and problems do not get solved. Rather, I encourage you to talk. Discuss things. Truth and love are wise guides for any communication.

So when you feel frustrated, first get yourself to a place where you are calm enough to think rationally. It is crucial that we each know how to calm ourselves down. What brings us comfort and allows for slow deep breathing and the ability to think clearly? When you get to that place, ask yourself some questions:

1. Am I tired, hungry, or hormonal?

   The smallest frustration can be blown out of proportion by us being out of whack. I have found myself not even aware of how tired, hungry, or hormonal I have been until I blow up at the slightest provocation. So take inventory of yourself before proceeding.

2. Ten years from now, will this matter? Ten days?

   Often when we can see things from a long-term perspective, it helps lessen the sense of urgency. If it's about disciplining the kids, then it deserves attention. If it's about your favorite towel that he used to wipe up his motorcycle grease, it's not worth a fight.

3. Is this something that is dangerous or unhealthy?

   If the frustration is about dirty socks left on the floor, you can let it go. If it's about him driving drunk, then it needs serious attention.

4. Are there creative options?

   Perhaps you can offer another solution that will avert a confrontation and help meet both your needs and his. You could buy him his own towels to use in the garage, and hide your good ones just to be safe.

One trick that has been helpful that I've been practicing saying out loud is, "It really doesn't matter." If I have realized that this will not matter in ten years, and that is it not harmful, it helps me let it go. By saying and hearing, "It really doesn't matter," my agitation level goes down. Try it. Kind of freeing, isn't it?

☙

35. How do I know if his addictions are intolerable or if I should just put up with them?

People who struggle with addictions and substance abuse usually struggle their entire lives. Some are victorious with much hard work, and others are not. When it comes to us, there is little we can do about another's addictions. Those who have participated in the Al-Anon program find helpful encouragement and support for themselves as they live with an addict. Our veterans who are desperate to be numb will struggle with addictions. Some drink. Some smoke pot. Others take excessive painkillers. Some overeat. Many find escape in porn. Others do hard drugs. Whatever their choice of "medication," it is destroying them and affecting all those who love them.

If their behavior is harming you or your family, you must take serious steps. If you are in danger, get out. Now—in the next five minutes. If it is just wearing you down and eating away at the relationship, you might consider an intervention. Carley was getting increasingly discouraged with Jack's drinking. At first she just tried to ignore it. And of course he denied having a problem. Every attempt to talk to him about it failed— especially when she got ticked off and they ended up fighting over it. That just drove him to drink even more.

One day he just begged her, "Can't you just accept me the way I am?" She was having a real hard time with that. But eventually she knew she either had to do something and see a change, or their relationship would be over. She also realized that her approach had been an attack rather than a plea. Carley had not been listening to her own self. She was not in touch with her fears. Down deep she was scared spitless. It frightened her to think of losing Jack, or worse, of seeing him gradually destroy himself. She realized she needed to communicate to him from a place of love and concern.

After talking with his adult children, they all agreed to meet together with him at a designated time and place, unbeknownst to Jack. She was very nervous, but knew she had no other viable options. The time came and they sat down with him. One at a time they each expressed their love and concern. She was able to convey to him that she loved him, she accepted him, but could no longer tolerate his destructive behavior.

That seemed to be the key to starting it out without triggering him. Love. Caring. True concern. Honesty. Hard to take, but deep down inside that is what we all long for. Much to her surprise, he was receptive. He gave it some thought and finally chose to take some steps in the right direction. Jack made some commitments and started working a program. And to this day they are actually doing really well. He will always struggle, but one day at a time he can be victorious. She continues to love and encourage him while going to the support group for herself.

We can't be there for our vets if we ourselves are isolated from our lifelines. Whatever their struggle, we bear it too. And we need each other to lean on. We need objective and practical support on an ongoing basis. Seek out a support group for the addictions and also for the PTSD. One motto for our Love Our Vets support group is, "Thanks for being there."

36. If he has a problem with addictions (such as alcohol), is it okay for me to drink?

It depends on your goal in life. What is your aim? What do you desire for yourself and for your vet and for your relationship and for your family? Sometimes we need to sacrifice one thing for a greater good. The payoff may be down the road. Can you drink in moderation and not harm yourself? Can you drink in moderation and not be a negative influence on him? Consider the people and the social environment. Are you going together to a place where it will be torture for him to resist? Or are you planning to drink all alone or perhaps with your friends only?

Dianne was very concerned with her vet's drinking addiction. Not only would he go on a binge, he'd also disappear for days. Usually she'd get a call form the VA detox a few days later where they were helping him get back on his feet temporarily. Her life was pretty miserable, but she just continued hanging in there with him. When he was sober he was wonderful. And those rare days were enough for her. The problem she struggled with was that she loved to go dancing with him and that involved drinking for both of them. She was not willing to give that up. Nor was she willing to go to Al-Anon or take him to AA. Finally, she admitted that she did not want to change her lifestyle, but she just kept hoping he would get better. Magically.

Rhonda was dating her vet with similar circumstances. He would drink, get angry, and then take off. She was tired of it all and realized she really wanted this to work—for the long haul. And she would do whatever it took to help him get sober—for good. She hated to give up her partying, but saw no other choice if she was to not undermine his efforts at sobriety. There have been ups and downs, but they are doing so much better now. She actually doesn't miss the partying, and together they have found other fun things to do. And better people to hang out with. When their children come along, I know they will be glad they've chosen the healthy path.

Everyone is different, and only you can decide what is best. It may be beneficial to talk it over with some wise people who can help objectively. We all need people like that in our lives who really care for us and have the courage to be honest.

✑❥

37. How do I know when to say something to him and when to hold it in? How do I weigh the benefit vs. the cost (backlash)?

I grew up in a family where it was not acceptable to speak your true feelings and opinions if they differed from those in charge. So it has only been recently (thanks to good counseling) that I have been learning to speak what I need to say without tremendous fear. It is a really healthy thing to be able to say what you need and want. Our vets also need to be encouraged to speak up and let us know what they need and want. And it goes without saying that these requests be done courteously.

But living with a PTSD vet, or even if we do not live with the vet we love, we have learned to often walk on eggshells and tiptoe around what we say. Sometimes a seemingly innocent comment or request may evoke a bombshell backlash. We ought to avoid any words that we know will provoke them, unless of course it is an issue of health or safety. If there is danger or it is really serious, then we must risk the backlash. Any words spoken can be bathed in love and gentleness and kindness. That will go a long way.

Also, I have learned that it is the first sentence that is the most important. The first sentence sets the stage for the rest of what you have to say. If you come across as angry or accusative or alarming in any way, the walls go up and you can kiss your communication good-bye. But if you can say what you need to say concisely and respectfully and use "I" messages, there will be a greater likelihood that it will be well received.

Here's another trick I have found helpful. I call it the "file folder." If something really bothers me but for whatever reason now is not a good time to bring it up, I file it mentally. Note I did not say to stuff it—nor ignore it. Just put it away for now. It leaves me feeling still in control with options, but I have used my good judgment to know that another time might be better.

The cool thing about it is that often in the next few days, I get more insight and better perspective on the subject. It also takes away the sense of urgency that I often impose on myself. I want to fix this now. Right now! Three days later I realize I survived, and often had time to arrive at a better solution. Or perhaps the thing resolved itself. In the meantime, there might be good opportunities to bring it up and discuss it with him. Sometimes just knowing that you can come back and revisit it is very helpful.

$$\mathcal{L}\!\blacktriangledown$$

38. How do I get him to "come back" to me when he is withdrawn or shuts himself off?

Holly's vet has said, "Sometimes I just want to run away and live in a cave all by myself. Just the TV and some donuts. I can watch TV, sleep, eat, and make all the disgusting bodily noises I want." Humorous as it may sound, the deep truth is that this is how they really do feel. And many of them actually do hide away in their "cave." Painfully shutting us out to heartbreaking loneliness.

Of all the symptoms manifested by PTSD, this one seems to be the most painful to those of us who deeply love our vets. The withdrawal and hiding behind walls and in caves can be so subtle it almost makes us question our own sanity more than theirs. Whatever it was that may have triggered them to retreat often eludes both them and us. All we know is that they are "gone." For some it is a physical separation. Abandonment. Or so it feels. For others it is emotional. Also abandonment.

We go back and forth trying to figure it all out and attempting to fix it all. At the same time, we wonder what we did wrong or what we could say to make it all better.

A better question to ask is how do I take care of me when he doesn't? Our job is not to "get him to come back." Our focus is to stay on our feet and continue living our healthy lives, doing our best to pour love on him even though it seems futile. How do I feel right now? Does my stomach feel like it's filling with acid? Or is the back of my neck about to snap in two from tension? Perhaps you just want to sit on the kitchen floor and weep. Just sob. Grieve. Maybe hit or kick a few things? Slam some doors?

Take the time to listen to what your heart is telling you. Hear yourself. Care for you. Comfort you. Now is the time to feel the feelings and then do something healthy for yourself. What do you need right now? When our loved one cannot give or care for us because he's disabled, we have to step up and nurture ourselves. As much as we desperately long for them to be there for us, we have to grieve the fact that they cannot do that for us. They would if they could. And somewhere deep inside of that warrior is a heart that is breaking because he cannot give us what we need.

Most of us have learned that eventually our vets do come back. The best thing we can do is welcome them home with open arms. Love them. Share with them how much we missed them and how much they mean to us. Once they have settled back into routine, it is okay and actually important that we share our pain with them. Let them know how hard it is for us when they are unresponsive.

Give them space and let them heal. And at the same time keep taking care of us. We have plenty of healing to do also. Perhaps eventually they'll start taking better care of themselves. But we cannot control that. We can do what is best for us, and love them. The better we take care of ourselves, the easier it is for them to come back. And they will.

39. How do I survive Veterans Day and other patriotic holidays?

A good start is to be prepared. Keep in mind that these days are like anniversaries. Fourth of July, Veterans Day, Memorial Day, etc. Even if our vets don't realize it, they do stir up stuff. Funny how a holiday looks like a party day to one person and a nightmare to another.

As wives and loved ones, we have to continually keep in mind awareness of our needs. What is going on inside of me? What is my stomach telling me? Why do I feel fearful today or angry? It isn't all about them. We must tend to ourselves first, and then we are in a better place to relate to them.

Jamie was dreading Veterans Day. Every year this cloud of gloom settled over their home and dampened everything. This year as usual, Harry was going to march in the parade with his unit. He was proud to be so patriotic and enjoyed the camaraderie. But the night after and the whole next week...month...season ..., he went into his hole—the dark, walled-off place where she couldn't touch him. She wished she could just fast-forward the calendar to Christmas, or spring...summer...well, at least after Fourth of July (which was even worse!). How about the month of August? There is usually a good week or two. Then it starts all over again.

Feeling hopeless? Trapped? Nothing to look forward to? Here are two things to consider. One thing we can do is communicate. Remember that the more we can connect with our vets, the more fulfilled they will be and we will be. Just sitting down and talking with them brings healing. Ask them questions. Let them know you are there. Listen. Care. Do they have pictures or memorabilia they want to show you? (A word of caution: This can aggravate PTSD.) Help them stay tuned to their feelings about these things. The more they can express their thoughts and feelings, the better it is for them too. And if you think it might help, encourage them to turn down any activities that get them stirred up in a negative way.

One vet decided that rather than sit around and relive the war, he would send Veterans Day cards to his friends. That really perked him up. Not only did he get his mind off himself, he was energized by reaching out to others. It was such a positive experience for him that he continues to do it every year.

What about you? Consider having fun. Who me? Fun? Yes, you. Remember you? Remember fun? Remember that creative side of you? Remember your pre-PTSD days? Get in touch with that alive part of you. What can *you* do to make this an enjoyable holiday for you? Plan a short out-of-town getaway, either for both of you or you alone. Or you and a couple of friends. Or the family without him. That is okay too. Throw a party if you want. Go to a party if you want. Go to the parade if you want. Be in the parade if you want.

Jamie chose to be creative. Instead of just waiting for the doom and gloom to begin, she planned a surprise for him. Funny thing: It was so much fun for her. She had three days to prepare. She bought a giant poster board and hid it from him, and devised a way to get to and from the parade without him knowing. Her creativity peaked as she designed her message on the poster when he wasn't home (had to air the house out because it smelled suspiciously like markers!). Then she figured out what to wear… her cutest cold-weather outfit. She wanted to look like a bombshell.

Parade day came and he left all anxious and grumbly as usual. She gave him a big hug and told him how proud she was of him. Then she got dressed in a flurry, grabbed her poster, and took off. She got a spot about halfway along the parade route. And there she stood. Her heart pounded like a schoolgirl with a crush. He'd be coming along any time now! This is crazy! She wondered why she was so excited and having so much fun. As she stood there waiting and holding her sign, she noticed the other bystanders and parade marchers were smiling at her. She proudly held up her red, white, and blue sign that read: "I really, really, really love my vet!" With hearts on it.

Soon she saw him coming. Her heart just pounded. As he came closer, she ran out into the middle of the street (yes, a parade crasher!), held up her sign, and gave him a big, long, wet kiss. Right there in the middle of the parade. His army buddies hooted and hollered and wanted a kiss too. The crowds cheered! It was the best parade entry they had seen yet.

It had been a long time since she had seen Harry smile like that. And he was still smiling that night and the next day. Two days later as they laid in bed, he said with moist eyes, "That was the nicest thing anyone has ever done for me. Thank you. I love you too." And that poster is still tacked up on the wall of his shop in the garage.

Jamie came alive. And as she came alive, so did her vet. It was a good Veterans Day.

40. I have a terrible time trying to sleep with him because of his nightmares and thrashing, etc. He has hit and kicked me several times too. How can I help him sleep better so I can sleep better?

If we don't get our sleep we are worthless. However, many of us have put ourselves last on the list of being cared for in the name of being loving. It has been our role to nurture others first and ourselves last. And sleep is seriously underrated in our culture.

Although PTSD affects everyone differently, most are affected greatly at night. Many vets deny they have a problem because during the day they seem fine. But look out for ni-nite time! Marcie's husband Bart was president of his military association and quite the outgoing happy-go-lucky guy. He was also about 6'5', and 350 pounds. She tried to talk to him about his wild sleep activities but he denied them—just laughed it off. Until the night he attacked her in his sleep and landed her in the hospital. Then he believed her and they both got help.

Jessica's boyfriend would wake up yelling and screaming every night. Once she woke up to a huge thud as he threw himself on the floor. A

huge tank crashed through the wall and almost ran them over! Then he
woke up. They got help too.

Dreams and nightmares are common. So is insomnia. Tossing and
turning can affect the bed partner just as much as yelling and thrashing.
Or if he is wide awake and wants to talk, or be funny (don't you just
hate it when you want to laugh but you're too tired?), or is feeling frisky
(starts squeezing things and talking cutesy…which we love at other
times!), when you desperately need your sleep. Then you feel like a bad
wife, and on it goes.

Although we can't fix them, there are a few things we can do. As
much as I hate to rely on drugs and medications when they are not necessary, this may be a time when his doctor can be of help. Encourage
him to examine his options. Most medications have both pros and cons
associated with them. There are also plenty of alternative medicine aids
out there for you to research. You might consider herbs or homeopathic
remedies or amino acids.

Also, the light box has been a great help to many. It's a broad-spectrum light almost identical to sunlight. It works best when used in the
morning for a little while every day, particularly in the dark winter
months. It helps reset the body's natural melatonin sleep cycle and also
improves seasonal affective disorder (depression due to lack of sunlight
and vitamin D). You can get them through the VA or online for a price
that is well worth it. Some of the rest of us benefit from that extra "sunlight" also. People like to read by the light when they first get up, or have
their coffee, or even do their workout.

If his sleep still doesn't improve enough for you to get yours, then
it's time to take care of you. What do you need to do to get a good night's
sleep? Do it. At one of our vet wives support groups we were astounded
when one lady admitted they do not sleep in the same room. Wow. That
is unheard of. How awful. What a failure. Loser. Actually, you could feel
an enormous sigh of relief rise up from the group! How many others had
been keeping that same little secret, thinking they were the only ones!
It's okay to sleep in separate beds or rooms. And if you're short on space,
the sofa can be very comfy. Or be creative. One lady set up an air mattress

and made a little bed on the floor of her closet.

Marcie was hesitant to do this, but she was so desperate. She felt like a failure, and he felt like she was "leaving him." It is important for both to have the discussion. "We both need our sleep. We do love each other. When we are unconscious, it really doesn't matter what bed we are in. It is the waking times that really matter. And if we can be better during our waking times, we can love each other that much more."

The quality of our marriages and relationships does not depend on who sleeps where at night. It depends on staying connected, close, loving, and communicative. Marcie and Bart worked it through and now have a new night-time routine that they both love. They go to bed together at the same time, naked. Yippee! Usually it's just time spent cuddling and talking about the day. Sometimes it gets lively and X-rated. Then they like to end the evening with a prayer before going to sleep. They have one last kiss, take out their teeth, and she goes to the other room for a good night's sleep.

Hard as it may be, we come to accept that our vets may never get good sleep. But that should never stop us from getting ours.

$\mathscr{L}$

41. How can I get to sleep when I'm ticked off?

Actually, we can't do much of anything well when we are over-the-top angry. Anger produces adrenaline in our bodies, which is pure energy. Fight or flight. Sorry, no sleep options there. It sure is a downer when we get angry at night. Been there. Seems so much more convenient if it was first thing in the morning, or just before a workout. Unfortunately we don't have the luxury of scheduling our anger. And when living with PTSD, it can flare up at any moment.

One of the things we as wives and loved ones of our vets need to learn and do well is to comfort ourselves and calm ourselves. We get plenty of opportunities to practice. And this has nothing to do with them. Just us. Our anger lets us know it's time to tend to our needs.

As annoying as they may be at times, our emotions are our friends. Even the unpleasant ones. Especially the unpleasant ones. Like pain, our body is sending us an urgent message. Something needs immediate attention. So the first thing to do is be aware. Stop. Get alone. Feel. Talk out loud if you want. "I feel so angry!" Name the feeling. Don't be too quick to explain it away or plunge into an activity to distract yourself. Stay with the feeling.

Tune into your body. Physically. What do you feel? Is your head pounding? Your stomach churning? Your neck tight? Your heart racing? They teach the vets with PTSD to do this too when they are triggered. Something about getting the brain back to a better place where you can think and feel, rather than in the place where you are triggered and "hijacked."

Next, just listen. Deep inside. Listen to you. Ask, "What do I need?" What am I missing that is making me cry out in rage like this? It could be that I need to be noticed and loved. Or I need space. I need quiet. I need time alone. I need sleep. I am hungry and need something nourishing. Honor yourself by listening.

Then examine your options. What are your healthy choices for meeting that need? What are your options for continuing to process the emotions? Often the two go hand in hand. As I take care of my needs, I am better able to sort through the thoughts and feelings; and as I sort through the thoughts and feelings, I am better able to make healthy choices in meeting my needs.

Kerry was really ticked off one night. She slammed doors, yelled, and went outside to try to cool off. At first she was not even sure what set her off. She was really angry. As she took a walk around the block, she began to think more clearly. Wow. It slowly became clearer that she was desperate for time alone and quiet. She had been with people all day and never got to take time to take care of herself. She was hungry and irritable. By the time she got back home, she was in a much healthier place. She had something good to eat, gave her husband a hug, and then told him she needed a little quiet time alone for a bit. She reassured him that it was not him, but just something she needed. (Side note: This is a very good idea. Our vets often jump to conclusions and that could set them off. Always try to talk to them calmly and reassure them that we're not abandoning them.)

What do you need to do right now that is good for you? Kerry got it. There are lots of healthy outlets, and in time you'll know what works best for you. Resist the urge to stuff your face with unhealthy comfort food, which will only bring you down further and make you more depressed the next day.

Tammy really struggled with this. Whenever she got triggered, she went to the kitchen and binged. Or got in the car and went to the nearest fast-food joint. Felt good at the time. Sort of numbed her. But after many years of too much weight gain, she finally started choosing other ways… healthy ways…to handle her anger. And she loves getting into her new jeans!

If it's anger, then you probably need to do something physical to get the energy out. Go for a walk. Or run. Don't drive while angry. I had a super-duper plastic Bart Simpson baseball bat. It was great therapy in times of rage. Lots of pillows and beds and walls got the snot beat out of them. (I lamented the day it finally popped. Need to put that on my Christmas list.)

Generally speaking, other healthy ways to process emotions might be journaling (you can use lots of #**!##@!!). Or doing something productive like cleaning. Or yard work. Or something creative like painting or needle-work. Hopefully you have a friend or two you can call in time of need.

But if it's at night and you need to calm down, there are a few other things to consider. The worst part is when your mind keeps circling and swirling and the anger goes nowhere. It only seems to gain momentum. You're stuck in the thought cyclone. You're beyond the point where thinking about it anymore is productive. So it's time to break the thought cyclone. Write down all you can and leave it until the morning. Put it in a literal file folder or drawer or Word document. Take solace in the fact that it will look different in the morning. And your brain will be more intact and able to see options. Right now you are stuck. You need to short-circuit your brain so it can calm down. Here are some things to try:

1. Read your material about PTSD (replaces self-pity with compassion).
2. Go to www.loveourvets.org for encouragement and support.
3. Clean out a drawer. (Use your energy to do something useful. It also utilizes the left brain so the right brain can simmer down.)
4. Send a note to someone who needs encouragement (gets your mind off you and on to someone else).
5. Go through old pictures (happy memories).
6. Read a funny book (it's okay to lighten up now).
7. Pray (connects you to God and adjusts perspective).
8. Listen to some soothing music (does not include acid rock or sad country-western).
9. Watch a fun or uplifting video or program.
10. Get caught up on emails or Facebook.
11. Soothe yourself with your favorite fragrance.
12. Do some research on the internet about a favorite subject.
13. Do some needlework or something calming with your hands.
14. Engage as many of your senses as you can (not counting the eating senses) such as smelling essential oils in a nice hot bath with candlelight.
15. Take some natural herbal remedies to calm you down, or have a cup of nice warm chamomile or lavender tea. Be careful not to get addicted to pharmaceutical sleep aids.
16. Love yourself. Massage your hands and feet.
17. Cuddle your cat or dog (actually rebalances the stress hormones in your body).
18. Breathe. Deep slow breathing. Very slow.
19. Meditate on something that is meaningful to you.
20. Give thanks. Count your blessings.
21. Tune in to your body, starting from the top of your head and work your way down. Feel everything.

Finally, be glad tomorrow is a new day. Things will look different then. Hang in there.

42. How do I know what his needs are and if I can help meet them?

Vets with PTSD have all the same needs as all human beings; and they have all the needs of men; and they have additional needs brought on by their trauma. Exactly what those are cannot necessarily be listed; however, a few we know are that they need to feel safe, need to have hope, and need to have meaningful connections with good people. Plus many need to have extra medical care, etc.

Have you ever asked him what his needs are? That might be a wonderful conversation. And one to have often. One thing I'm learning is that conversations don't need to be concluded in one sitting; they can be continued, revisited in phases, or even layers. Our communication can be linear or at times like peeling an onion…so stay open and let time work. He may not even be aware of his needs at first. But the more you can connect together, the more those needs can be addressed.

As far as our role in meeting those needs—whatever our relationship with them—it really varies. Unfortunately, many of us want to find a "quick fix" in meeting their needs, as if we had that power. We do not. And there is no fix, quick or otherwise. But there is love and comfort and understanding, which all go a long, long way.

One more key thought: When we as wives and loved ones focus on taking care of ourselves in healthy ways, we are in a much better position to support them.

43. He is drawn to war movies. Should I discourage him from watching them because it seems to not be helpful at all?

It seems odd to me that the thing that traumatized them is the very thing that draws them back. War intrigues them. Actually, it does most people to some degree, but for the PTSD vet it seems to have a mysterious enticement. I wonder if they are drawn to it because it's familiar down deep, or if perhaps they feel somehow they can conquer it. Like a moth is drawn to a flame, our vets are ironically attracted to violent re-enactments. Something inside them resonates with it and desperately longs to "fix" the problem by reliving it in some form. Most vets prefer to watch war movies and documentaries where they know the good guys win. Others may be fixated on playing video games where they can conquer and obliterate the evil guys.

Still, the whole idea of war and death are disturbing no matter who "wins." It doesn't seem to benefit them in any way. In fact, it most likely stirs things up and causes much agitation, either conscious or subconscious.

The best thing we can do is connect with them. If you can handle it, watch it with him. Personally, I cannot watch war movies. They disturb me. I have to take care of me and leave the room. Whether you watch it with him or not, you can talk about it. Have a discussion. It may be a good inroad to encourage him to talk. It is good to share our concerns with them and then to honestly ask, "I don't understand why you like those disturbing movies. I would think that would stir things up. Can you help me understand what intrigues you about them?"

Our job is not to fix or change, but we are privileged to be close enough to love them and connect. If they choose to open up at any level, that is a beautiful thing for both. And any discussion does not require a mutually agreed-upon solution. What a freeing concept! I remember the first time someone told me that. You mean we don't have to solve everything at the time we discuss it? Every topic can be revisited at another time…especially if one or both are triggered or upset. Sometimes we just need to think about things over time. Any thought seeds planted can often prove to be helpful later.

Another idea is to offer something else that would be uplifting and beneficial. Whenever we have to remove something from our lives, it is most effective when we can replace it with something better. Otherwise there remains a vacuum, a hole that will often be refilled by something not so good, or the original thing comes back. So here I date myself: I went online and bought a bunch of DVDs of shows we both enjoyed way back. Mr. Ed, I Dream of Jeannie, and Get Smart! How fun! We both get a kick out of these and it's really good to see something wholesome and entertaining. We are left smiling and feeling good. (Feeling old too, but that's okay).

44. How much power do I have to keep things from escalating when we start a conflict?

More than you realize! That good news carries relief but also responsibility. As loved ones who are not burdened directly with PTSD, we have more power than we realize.

Janessa and Larry had a history of going at it—often. He would rant and she would rave. In no time at all they were hosting their own private war inside their home. Not pretty. And it left a wake of debris in their relationship. Not to mention how it was harming their children. After listening to some of the other wives share what has worked for them, she decided to give it a try. The next time she felt the urge to attack him, whether in defense or initiating the assault, she planned to just hold it in. The first time she tried this she failed. The second time she was caught off guard because it was a subtle sneak attack—not easily identified. But finally, she got to see it work.

One evening, he was triggered by a military commercial on TV. Unfortunately, he ended up exploding all over her. As much as she wanted to blast right back, she fought the urge. She told him she was not going to talk until he calmed down. Trembling, she walked out of the room and called a friend. A while later he came to her and apologized. Not every story will end so peacefully, but at least now they know it's possible.

It has been said that it takes two sides to have a war. If only one person is fighting, there will be no war. In every relationship, conflict is inevitable. But if one person can contain the ammunition and remain neutral, thus preventing the battle and keep it from escalating, then the other person has a chance to calm down—before things are said and people are hurt.

If we can contain our rage and emotions that often get triggered and work through them alone, often he will settle down on his own. And both of us will settle down. When I act in the emotion of the moment, it backfires or more likely explodes like a nuclear bomb. Then it becomes something way out of our control and can last for days or weeks.

But if we realize how much power we actually do have to contain the potential fireworks, then we need not indulge in spilling our guts, which will only fuel the fire to outrageous proportions. The first step is to be aware of when our feelings start to boil. What is that chill up my spine? Or that tension headache? Why am I clenching my teeth again? Then choose to do something healthy, a distraction or positive replacement for that negative emotion. Sometimes it may just be removing myself from the situation like Janessa did by going into another room. Or for some it may be a distress call for help to God. Now is a good time for divine strength and grace.

The good thing about that approach is when we get alone, we have the opportunity to think and process our emotions and get a more objective perspective on the situation. This time alone will often help us sort through and distill down what we really need and want. Then we're able to speak it in a better way that will be better heard by him. It takes a few times of blowing it to realize it's not worth it to explode. It is well worth it to hold it in temporarily and work it through on our own, and then communicate in kindness with him later. There would be no wars if one side was neutral. It takes two to fight.

∅

45. How do I say the things I need to say in a way that he can hear?

Our PTSD vets are programmed for protection. The enemy is always lurking. So with the slightest hint of danger or attack, up go the walls. The fortress. And out come the weapons. With that always in mind, how can we talk to them without tripping the alarms? We must learn to communicate in a way that makes them feel safe. Loved. Respected. Empowered.

Julia was at her wits' end. "No matter what I say to Jed, he says I am controlling him. I can't even make suggestions or ask for anything without him getting all ticked off." Megan's husband would often respond defensively by telling her that she is always putting him down. From his perspective, no matter what he does he can never please her. So both women wondered how they could ever ask for anything or make a suggestion.

Other family members have expressed frustration from instances when they said something and he literally could not hear it. Or when they inquired about it at a later time, he had no idea what she was talking about. Literally put up walls of deafness. Feeling quite helpless, we wonder, "Do we just shut up and never talk again?"

One thing to keep in mind is that our vets were alive before their trauma. Many of them already had baggage going into the war. The trauma only intensified what they already struggled with. It is helpful in understanding them and loving them to take into consideration all their issues, pre- and post-war. When Julia began to reflect on what Jed had told her about his upbringing, she remembered that his mother was extremely controlling. She sucked the life out of him. Then add a few Army officers kicking him around. Throw in life-and-death survival mode and horrific trauma—and there you go. You have a man who reacts to what he perceives as a threat: being controlled.

Megan's husband grew up in an alcoholic home where the father was quite abusive. And according to both parents, he was never good enough. Never lived up to his potential. Always put down. Belittled. Not worth a hill of beans. Add a military trauma and a wife who just makes an innocent comment, and he is back in the war.

Isn't it good to know that it really is not our fault? It's not a matter of just being a better wife, partner, loved one, or friend. So let's relax for a

moment. Take time to reflect on his pre-war traumas. Get a good understanding of his baggage. (We have ours too!) It does take conscious effort
and practice, but keeping it in mind always will be worth the trouble.
Eventually it will come more naturally.

The bottom line is to communicate in a way that does not trigger
him. We have the power to sort through our emotions and distill it down
to a place where we can use words and tones that they can hear. That
will probably mean no more spontaneous blurting out of what's on our
mind at the moment. We do not have that luxury. It may also mean no
speaking out the whole truth of all we feel at a given moment. (Rats!)
Aren't we women supposed to be able to emote freely? Nope. Not if it
causes walls. Or war.

We have the power to think through what we want to communicate—and then to express it in love, kindness, and respect. We do have
the right and the responsibility to say what we need and want, but need
to do it with grace and quiet calm strength.

Another way to effectively communicate with them is to use questions.
When asked with wisdom and love, questions can be wonderful tools.
Good for stimulating our vets to think, to feel empowered when we ask
their input, and to feel respected. Questions allow time for response and
should not feel like an attack. Questions do not corner; they set free.

Another helpful tool is to remember to use "I" and "we" statements
rather than "you." Talking about what I feel or I need, or a problem we
have, is much less threatening than starting off with a big fat "you" statement. It's really important to incorporate that strategy into our communication. And it works. Starting with "I" opens up the communication
regardless of whose needs are being expressed.

Shelby's vet was in a funk about a legal mess he was facing. Intending
to be helpful, she barged right in telling him what she thought he should
do, graciously offering her opinion. Not what he wanted to hear. It triggered him instantly. Walls up. "I do not want to talk about it!" Of course,
her feelings were hurt. But as she calmed herself down and reminded
herself that this was not about her, she was able to see more clearly what
they both needed. After giving it more thought (in another room), she

realized what he really did need to hear.

Waiting until he calmed down a bit, she approached him with a gentle hand on his arm. Knowing she only had about two seconds before he shut her out, she got right to the point. "If I were in your shoes, I would feel the same way. I am praying for you." Short. Simple. Supportive. She gave him a kiss and went to go lie down. He must have heard her because when she got up from her nap, there was a bouquet of flowers waiting for her on the kitchen table.

Our goal is to stay connected. We can be strong and loving on the inside, as well as outwardly through our words, tone of voice, and actions.

46. Sometimes he has a hard time making decisions. Either he commits too readily then later resents it, or he feels trapped as if he has no choices. How can I help him when he has to make a decision or when we have to make one together?

PTSD causes a person to often feel panicked, cornered, and in survival mode. So when it comes to decisions, sometimes the brain just cannot access the logical part. So they either jump too quickly, or freeze. What I've found to be most helpful are two things: questions and gently presented options. We can help them sort through the confusion as long as we stay calm and gentle.

First, what questions can you ask him that will guide him to the best decision? Sharon and Joe were agonizing over whether or not to buy a certain car. He was literally tormented. It helped them both when she was able to distill it down to the most important factors. With paper and pencil in hand, she asked him to list the absolute essential things the car must have and what features it would take to make him feel comfortable buying it. The next list was what he would like to have in a car but could be flexible about. It didn't take long for him to see more clearly. They bought the car—not without quite a bit of nervousness, which is okay. And, she reports happily, they still have that car and love it.

One thing to keep in mind is that before we go butting in, it never hurts to ask if they're open to our thoughts. Or to ask if he minds if we ask a few questions to help him in his decision process. It all boils down to respect. We're supporting them in their decision and helping them with what they want and need. And believe it or not…brace yourself: We do not always know what is best for them! (For those of us who like to control and fix, it keeps us humble!) Never be afraid to admit we don't know everything, and always be willing to learn something new each day.

Another part of helping them is to show them they do have options. PTSD sees no options. The trauma leaves a person feeling out of control. It is so empowering when they realize they actually do have control over their lives in many ways. Things are not always black or white, yes or no. There are many options in between. Jason was very stressed over a decision about purchasing another gun. At first he was extremely anxious and overwhelmed. But Molly encouraged him to take his time and get more information. Examine his options. After it was all over, he remarked to her, "Information is power." And he thanked her for her helpfulness. (By the way, they now have a fourteenth gun.)

Cynthia recalls the morning her vet was frustrated at the toaster because the knob was not working right. "As I started to go into 'fix mode' with ideas of things we could try, he suddenly blurted out, 'I'll just take it outside and shoot it!'" That was a comical reminder that we do have the ability to help them see options, and they do not just have to jump off the ledge of hopelessness.

We can also help them learn the trick of not giving an answer on the spot, but instead tell the person they will think about it and get back to them. How freeing! That way they have time to sort things though and feel more confident when they finally make their decision. I know that for me, time always opens up new possibilities and ways of looking at something. And if anyone pressures me to make a decision on the spot, I walk away. Remember to give lots of hugs and verbal support. One of their fears is not doing things perfectly and being rejected. We all like to be reassured that if we make a wrong decision, we will still be loved. And we will survive; we will be okay.

One more thing that I have seen very helpful is prayer. Any time you as a couple or family can pray together, it establishes a deeper connection among all involved. No special words are needed. Just heart. I can't explain it, but I know it works. Something about acknowledging our need for God and tapping into His resources. Worth a try.

⟡

47. How do his "anniversaries" affect him? Affect me?

His anniversaries are memories—whether fully conscious or not—that take him back into his trauma. For some, these dates are clear, horrible, and devastating. For others, there is a gloomy fog hanging over them that they just can't identify. And every range in between. Some may last a day. Others months. You may see a familiar pattern every year, or it may be different each year. But as nebulous and unformulated as they are, they still wreak havoc for both the vet and those around him. Sometimes the veterans are not even aware of what took place back then, but they react annually anyway. It seems as though the body remembers even when the brain has blocked it out.

Erin's vet was recently diagnosed with PTSD. It was all new to both of them. Neither of them even knew about anniversaries. One day they were having an ugly argument in the kitchen about the kitchen. Both were contributing and it escalated instantly. Yelling and name-calling. (Erin was overwhelmed and fearful and angry and wanted it all to stop but could not and wondered where it all came from to start with—all these thoughts running through her mind in a split second.) Suddenly he blurted out, "It's the Marines' birthday!" What? Huh? Erin was stunned. Both went silent. He stormed out of the room. Then it dawned on her. This was not about the kitchen at all. It was about an anniversary. The good news is that they have both connected with good support and help. She made a note on her calendar to be ready next year and to address it in advance with him. Use it as an opportunity to talk, to be close, and to connect and heal. By the way, the kitchen is great.

The best thing those of us who love them can do is first to support them and then to be sure to take care of ourselves. Reach out in love and concern. Connect with them before and during these times. Another vet wife, Lydia, noticed her vet had been acting unusually irritable and depressed for several days. She started noticing that she too began to feel irritable and depressed. One morning, rather than getting ticked off and starting a fight (which she really felt like doing), she took several slow deep breaths to calm herself down. Then she went in, wrapped her arms around him, and told him how much she loved him. She opened up to him by saying that she had been feeling a little irritable and depressed and also that he seemed to be too. She asked if he was coming near to an anniversary. He paused, thought a minute and then said, "You know, I hadn't thought about that but you're right. Tomorrow is the fourteenth and that was the day I enlisted." She encouraged him to talk more if he felt like it— which he did and let out a whole bunch of steam we cannot print here!

It's often a relief to the vets to logically see a "reason" for their disturbances. In a way it helps them feel they're truly not going crazy after all.

Lydia chose to love. She started by affirming him and then making herself vulnerable by disclosing her feelings. But then she stayed in her healthy place and "held on to herself" as she reached out to him.

Consider sitting down with your vet, pen and paper in hand. Ask him if he would be willing to go back into his past, as difficult as that can be, and share with you the significant events along the way. Let him know that you want to be there with him and for him all through the seasons, and it would be helpful to you to have it written down as a reminder. Lovingly hold him or his hand as you journey together through some of the darkness. Listen, encourage, comfort. Don't fix. Ask questions if that would be helpful to him. This journey into the sequestered recesses of his mind will likely trigger him, set him off, or affect his mood. That is okay. Your presence by his side will touch him deeply and soothe the inner wounds. This time will also bring you both closer together.

In addition to seeing our vets suffer because of the past, the hardest part is keeping ourselves separate from them and not taking on their moods. We should not be surprised that we too are affected. As these anniversaries approach, acknowledging and talking about how we both feel is really good. There is something freeing about just owning our feelings. Not having to fix our feelings. Not judging them. Just owning them. We need to be especially cognizant of our own downward pull during these times. We need to be especially aware of our needs and be diligent to take care of ourselves. And it is always a help to remember that the dates do pass.

48. How can I enjoy the good times, knowing that he may change at any moment? Do I always have to keep my guard up?

A wonderfully freeing concept came to me recently. Seems so simple. But it has taken me many years to get this one: I am not required to keep anyone happy. Wow! Really? How many of us are driven, enslaved to do all we can to keep everybody happy? Well, the good news is that first we do not have to. And second, even if we did have to, we can't! Hard as we may try, we cannot keep everyone (or anyone) happy. Not possible. (Even God does not try to keep everyone happy!)

So that frees me up to enjoy him just as he is. To enjoy being me, just as I am. Goofy. Imperfect. Loving. Learning. Growing. We do have good times. Really good times. And we long for more. But we also know that the bad days come along just as well.

I am free to let my guard down. I must, in order to feel the good times. The temptation to stay numb and safe is always there. Just as it is with the vets. But if I am to experience the joy in life, I need to take that risk. Freedom to feel joy carries with it the risk of pain. But I would rather feel joy and pain than not feel at all. That is not living. That is being trapped. That is my internal death if I cannot be free to feel and free to take a risk.

His mood changes are his. He cannot dictate how I feel. If I let him dictate my feelings, then I'm not healthy. Also, I've found that when I am free and fun and alive, he is more likely to pick up on that than if I stay guarded. Life can be contagious!

And remember that we cannot expect to get all we need from any one person—not even our vet. That is why God gave us friends.

✿

49. Sometimes I feel like I'm married to Dr. Jekyll and Mr. Hyde. Is that typical, and how do I manage with those extreme and unpredictable behaviors?

Yes, it is typical. Ups and downs and sideways and zigzags…all part of the disorder. And also typical for us to do our own zigzagging along with theirs. Sometimes we feel resentful about it, like we're being jerked around by their instability. Is it possible to feel like you're in love with two or even more distinct people? In the movie *Dr. Jekyll and Mr. Hyde*, the wonderful brilliant good doctor turned into an evil cruel frightening "man." Back and forth between the two extremes.

When Darlene was dating Jeff, she kept searching for the "real Jeff." Where was he? Which of these guys was the real man she loved? The old TV show "To Tell the Truth" kept playing in her mind. Why was he so loving and calm one day and the next he was in a rage or deep depression? Why was he the hit of a social occasion one day and hiding in his cave the next?

Rita was part of a Love Our Vets support group. She often expressed her pain and frustration about Doug, particularly when it came to relating to their children. He was nice some of the time, but more often impatient and angry with them. One evening, one of the other ladies happened to see Rita and her family at a local restaurant. After introducing each other's families, they talked for a few minutes and went their separate ways. At the next meeting, the other lady expressed her surprise. "Doug was really nice. He didn't come across at all as angry or impatient." Of course, Rita was happy about that. We all want our men to make us proud in public. But at the same time she also felt alone, frustrated that the other lady may not have believed her. We all assured her that we definitely understand the Dr. Jekyll/Mr. Hyde quandary.

We understand it in that we live with it; however no one really understands it. Once again we are grappling with a frustration we cannot fix. Yet still we seem to be driven to understand these enigmas with the hope that if we could figure it out, then we could solve it. Sorry. There is no fix.

But we *can* keep on loving them and taking care of us. Rita was on the right track by staying connected with others who were a positive support. In the ups and downs, we need to be anchored to something/someone good who will help provide health and stability. Good people to talk with. Good input to read. Enough faith (it doesn't take much) to connect with God. And a keen awareness of what we need.

How do his mood swings affect us? Physically, what do I feel in my body? For some it is a sick stomach, tight shoulders, or forgetting to breathe. For others it may be a headache, pounding heart, or sudden fatigue. The more we can tune in to what our body is trying to tell us, the better we will be able to grow stronger in the chaos.

Some call it grounding. Others refer to it as centering. Or perhaps anchoring. Whatever you need to do to support you, in spite of his turmoil, do it. Take the time to take care of you.

Another thing we can do is to remember that they have PTSD. Initially, Ali was very enthusiastic about connecting with our group. Her fiancé Gavin was having a really hard time. She found great help and encouragement from sharing and learning with the others. But eventually when things got better she stopped coming. Her email read: "We are doing great. Gavin is doing very well. I am so busy and I don't really need the support like I did before. Thank you so much for being there and helping so many people." That was before he came to his anniversary month. Then Mr. Hyde showed up again. Thankfully, Ali came back.

When our vets do well, they do very well. Sometimes we can get lulled into the comfort of feeling like everything is normal. They are better. We subconsciously assume that it will keep going that way. That is our dream. Only to be rudely awakened without warning. Then we remember. Oh yeah, PTSD. And the vicious cycle goes on. Keeping in mind that their PTSD will always affect them at some level is not putting up a wall, but just being realistic. When we know what to expect, it doesn't knock us off our feet so easily. It still hurts, and it's still scary. But we can do just fine even if they are not.

℘

50. Is it important for me to frequently and truthfully tell him that I'm glad to be married to him?

Yes. Important for you and for him. And you'll find that the more you do it, the more you'll feel it. Our vets are riddled with self-doubt and insecurity. Although they may have a hard time expressing it, they long for your love and approval. They like to come across as tough and self-sufficient, but deep down inside they are like every other human being. We all need to be loved and wanted.

Your husband needs to know he's making you happy, at least on some level. I don't encourage you to lie, especially if there are issues you both need to address. But seek to be grateful for every thing you can, no matter how small. And take the time to tell him. It will make you feel good and will touch him more than you realize.

And just food for thought: Am I being the kind of wife that he is happy to be married to?

℘

51. What are boundaries and are they important for relationships with PTSD?

There are many outstanding books on this subject, but I will try to give a nutshell version. Colleen shared with us that watching her mother over the years taught her a tough lesson. Her mother could never say "no," always wanting to please people—often at her own expense or that of her family. Eventually, she had a nervous breakdown. Ironic isn't it, that at that point all she could say was "no." When you collapse you are no good to anybody, not even yourself. Colleen has learned to say "no." And she is doing great. And people don't hate her! Wow.

Boundaries are a clear and gracious way of protecting yourself and your time so you can be your best for the people and activities that are most important to you. It may be turning down a social activity in order to have a little time alone or more sleep. It may be turning off your cell phone for awhile. It may be saying "no thank you" to a charity event so you can reserve your energy for the other volunteering you do. It may be that you feel like you're going to go crazy if you don't get a little time alone.

Monica thought she was about to lose it. Whenever she went into the bathroom, the kids would barge in or call out to her. Her husband also didn't seem to notice that there was a door. Even the dog liked to join her. Really fun for everyone! Until one day it occurred to her that she could lock the door. She clearly announced to everyone that when she was in the bathroom, they would have to wait until she came out. She told them she would be happy to talk to them when she came out, but that while she was in there, she needed some privacy. At first they didn't believe her. She kept the door locked and graciously repeated what she had said. Eventually they began to respect that closed door. But she was the one who needed to put up the boundary. The dog still doesn't get it.

At the other extreme, it may be a more serious issue of safety. Amanda was living with her vet when he got extremely angry. She locked herself in the bathroom. He was so enraged he pounded and pounded and finally broke the door down. Miraculously, she managed to get out that night. Unfortunately, she returned two days later. As I listened to her story, I asked her about boundaries. She responded with a puzzled look, "What are boundaries?" Amanda had a lot to learn about the okay-ness—the necessity!—of protecting yourself. If words don't stop the abuse, then you need to get out.

Whether it involves blatant intrusion into our very lives or just annoying interruptions, healthy boundaries are our friend. Our lives can get so complicated and overly busy that we run the risk of burning out. Take some time to think about who and what are truly the most important to you. Then perhaps who or what you can eliminate. Saying "no thank you" without giving a reason is a life skill we all need. We owe no one any explanations, and even if you try they'll argue with you. So it is best to just make your statement graciously and leave it at that.

(I do encourage you to read more about this!)

℄♥

52. How do I draw a line with him in what is acceptable behavior toward me? And how do I have a backup for if he crosses the line?

You have to draw it now—before it becomes urgent. Take time to think through the last few months. What behavior toward you needs to stop? What has he done or said that is dangerous or unacceptable for you? Perhaps he's cursing at you in anger. Or maybe grabbing you? Or threatening you or your children in any way?

Now is not the time to make excuses for him. If you start to do that, stop—right now. Our tendency is to protect our vets and also our dreams of who we wish they were. Holding out for the dream, or convincing ourselves that he will change, leads to a dead end. It's not good for you or for him. How does it help him if you cover for his bad behavior? Denial feels better, but leads to destruction. So be honest.

Identify the specific behavior you will not tolerate. Do not speak in generalities. Be very specific. Practice what you will say. When the time comes, there will be a flurry of emotions and it will be helpful to be prepared. If he yells at you, stop right then. Look at him. Do not say it in fear or anger (although you'll be trembling and your heart is pounding). Then speak clearly. Whatever you have decided beforehand to say, do it now. "Please do not yell at me." Or, "That tone of voice is unacceptable." Or, "Do not curse at me."

Then be prepared for a backlash, but do not match his anger. If necessary, repeat what you said calmly. Or just leave the room. Go to your safe place. Call someone if you can. It really helps to talk about it and to get reassurance that you are not evil or hormonal.

Trina's husband was fixing some plumbing in their bathroom—specifically the toilet. Fixing toilets is never fun for anyone, let alone someone with PTSD. Remember their tolerance for stress is almost always filled to capacity. Well, something went awry and so did he. He flew off the handle and lashed out at her in anger. (All she was doing was folding laundry.) Since this was not the first time, she was ready. She looked up at him (he is much bigger than she and suddenly became especially bigger at that moment). Mustering up her courage, but still quaking, she said, "I know you're upset, but it is unacceptable to yell at me." And she left the room. And she made a phone call to one of her vet wife friends.

You will notice, as Trina did, that the more you speak clearly what is unacceptable, the more courage you have to do it the next time. I wish I could guarantee that it would always accomplish what you ask for, but we all know that the other person's response is not our responsibility. Hopefully in time they will grow and learn. Although some of us may not see it often, at the root of our vets' hearts is a keen desire to please us. The more connected they are to God in faith and to us in love, the more progress we will see.

In the meantime, all we can do is speak our needs and then stick by our request. If we ask for no yelling or hitting and they continue to do it, we need to have a plan. Tell them the next time they do that (be specific) you are going to _____ (be specific). And then do it. If you threaten to leave and stay with a relative, then pack your stuff (or have it ready) and do it.

For those who are in danger, you need to have a plan in place way before the crisis. I urge you to make some calls and find a shelter or a friend where you can go at a moment's notice. Or your situation may warrant a restraining order. Take the time to find a reputable attorney or social service that can help you with this vital protection if necessary.

It is time to take care of ourselves. And interesting to note that the more we take care of ourselves, the better they seem to get.

53. Why do I tend to make excuses for him, starting in my own mind?

It's all about the dream. What we wish versus what we live. We are fixers, problem-solvers, courageous, and ever hopeful. And we love our vets. Most of us can envision them the way we long for them to be. Perhaps we draw on past memories pre-PTSD. Janie was best friends with Zach all through high school. They fell in love and grew up together. They got married just before he went on his tour to Iraq. He never came back. The person who came back in his body was not the same Zach everyone knew and loved. Janie still longs for things to be the way they were. She feels guilty and torn as she struggles to accept him as he is, while dreaming of the good old days.

Denial feels good. Actually it does not feel. It is numb. When we don't face reality, but make excuses for ourselves or our vets, we are not living. True fulfillment comes from facing the truth and going from there.

Counseling for yourself, for him, for both of you together, and for your family will be very important. Cherish the memories. And hold on to the dream that lies ahead. Many of us have seen our vets transformed. But growth has to start with the truth.

54. His guns in the house scare me. What can I do?

The most important thing is safety. Do all you can to ensure that you and your family are not in danger. We are not always able to control our vets, but there are some things in our power. For starters, you can insist that all guns stay locked up. There are excellent gun safes available for a price that is well worth it. Be sure you and he agree on where the key will be kept—someplace not accessible to your children.

Also, it's good to agree that all guns are unloaded unless in use. No loaded guns around the house. Decide together on the safest place to keep ammunition and a safe place to clean and repair the guns.

Those are basic safety measures that should not be too hard to maintain. Beyond that, you can always request more drastic measures, but do not expect compliance. It is helpful for us to understand why guns are so important to our vets. Jessica was frantic about Gabe's ever-growing gun collection. He seemed to never be able to be satisfied. Always buying more guns and more ammo. He was good about keeping them locked up and put away whenever there were other people at the house. But always in the back of her mind she envisioned a mishap, or worse, a deliberate suicide. He just got agitated whenever she nagged him about it. And it did no good.

Eventually Jessica attended a PTSD information class, which was very helpful in shedding some light on Gabe's thinking. Our vets plagued with PTSD are tormented day and night with endless fear. At any moment they could be attacked. Ambushed. The enemy lurks everywhere. Never let your guard down. Weapons provide a sense of protection. Security. Defense. For them and for you. And this probably will go on until the day they die. What an awful thing to have hanging over your head at all times. No wonder they find comfort in carrying a gun. And amassing them.

In that class she heard many stories of soldiers from both recent and past conflicts. One Vietnam veteran, who currently owns more than forty guns, complete with thousands of rounds of ammo, shared his story. When they were deep in the jungle and under enemy attack, they ran out of ammo and also had a malfunctioning gun. Coming back for more bullets and a gun that worked, they were denied. Those young, brave, terrified soldiers were ordered to return to combat with no more bullets and guns that wouldn't protect them. Even now, he continues to collect more bullets and guns on a regular basis.

On her learning curve, another thing Jessica decided to consider was taking a firearms safety class. The more we can learn about firearms, the safer we will be. It might also be a good idea to include your kids if they are an appropriate age. Sometimes our fear can get blown out of proportion. Knowing more not only is helpful practically, but it's also reassuring.

Gabe was thrilled that Jessica wanted to learn more. And when she got her concealed weapon permit, he was on cloud nine! For her birthday he bought her a little pistol and took her out target shooting. He glowed as he complimented her: "You have the eye of a hawk!" Funny how she kind of even began to enjoy it.

Be safe. Be smart. And maybe even have some fun.

55. What is my part in monitoring or weighing in on his medications?

Whenever a bunch of women get together, especially in a restaurant, the other people probably wish they had stayed home. We women have the wonderful capacity of laughing and crying and everything in between. One particular evening was just like that. Several of us who love our vets got together. The conversation revolved around our husbands' medications. One would have thought we were medical professionals the way we bantered about the lists of their meds, and where to keep the updated lists, and how often to update it, and what was that? Oh, the doctor changed from this to that but still monitoring this but a little more of that and in a transdermal patch instead of oral, and his blood sugar was over 360, and on and on. We did draw the line when one lady began discussing the details of her husband's bathroom habits. (At least not during dinner anyway.)

The common need was being overwhelmed with all the complications of his meds and struggling with how much we should be involved. Each person and relationship and case is unique. But the underlying principles still are helpful. Whenever possible, let the medical professionals do their job. We can be helpful to our vets by encouraging them to go to their scheduled appointments and take their prescribed medications. We do need to stay informed and have ongoing current information regarding their medications and health. Some even recommend carrying that info in our purse and also a copy in his wallet.

But in some cases when our observations and intuitions signal a problem, then we need to act on it. We know our vets better than anyone and can tell if there are detrimental side effects occurring. Get more information, whatever that entails. The medical professionals are not infallible. They do not know everything. And sadly, in some cases, they have only enough resources to move the vets in and out as if they were on an assembly line.

Tory was at her wit's end. She and Darrin had been struggling and were on the verge of divorce. He was suicidal, angry, depressed, and abusive. And it just kept getting worse. Counseling didn't help either of them. Finally she got him to go to the doctor for an assessment. Amazingly, the doctor took him off most of his meds and adjusted the others. Within a few days he was a different man. The joy and love and calmness had returned. It had been the improper medications that were destroying him.

It's good for us to stay up on these things without letting them consume us. Ultimately our vets are responsible for their medications, unless they are totally dependent. And if that is the case, then hopefully they have a case manager to oversee those issues.

In the meantime, circumstances may arise when it would be advantageous for both our vets and our own peace of mind to personally and directly communicate with the doctor(s). We are here to love, support, and encourage, and to occasionally do some research and advocacy on their behalf.

And by the way, let's not neglect our own health issues!

56. Where is the fine line between owning my own stuff and lying down and taking abuse?

One of the most common traits we have seen in the women who attach themselves to vets with PTSD and stay in an abusive relationship is low self-esteem. "I'm not worth much. I should be glad to have a man, even if he doesn't treat me like a lady." Or thinking like this: "It was my fault. I shouldn't have said or done what I did. I just brought it on myself. I will do better next time."

At the opposite extreme (neither of which is healthy) is the person who denies any responsibility at all. "It's all his fault. I'm pretty wonderful, and he just blows up at me for no reason at all." Perhaps somewhere in the middle is the healthiest place.

We all have our faults and our baggage. Just comes with being born here on planet earth. The difference is that those who are healthy will see the truth and learn from it. That is called growth. It is good. Very good! May we never stop growing. At the same time, a healthy person will also recognize abuse—and not put up with it. The goal is to be healthy enough to see and own our weaknesses, and also recognize bad behavior in others and have healthy boundaries with them.

Kara was torn to pieces about her husband threatening to leave. She told us that he slammed her against the wall on several occasions. She was encouraged to take her kids and get out and to go to a safe place *now*. She said she couldn't do that because she loved him. And he really didn't mean it. But she was totally baffled at why he had changed so much. She didn't see anything that she was doing as provoking him. And she refused to go to counseling for herself.

The next week her husband was overheard in our small community saying that she was just a (insert choice word) and he had put up with it for too long. He admitted that he didn't treat her right but that she deserved it. He, too, refused to go for counseling.

Somewhere between these two conclusions is probably the truth. They both had issues to work on and they both needed to learn to behave more lovingly. Sounds simple, but we all have to start somewhere. No person, no matter who they are or what they've done or not done, deserves to be mistreated. It is our place and privilege as loved ones to initiate the kindness. And the truth. We have the power to make some healthy changes if necessary. Grace and truth—a perfect combination. We begin by taking an honest look at our behavior and where we need to improve. Then, we also take an honest look at what behavior is not acceptable toward us and take a stand against it. As one person put it, "We put up with too much bad behavior. We gotta have some limits."

The more we stand up for ourselves and also fight for the good in this relationship, the better we will feel about ourselves, and the result will be an improved and growing relationship. And won't it be great to have our man talk about us to his vet buddies with really good words? Hopefully we will do the same.

✍

57. I don't know how much longer I can keep doing this. How do I know when to say I'm done?

That is the hardest question we have asked ourselves at one time or another. It hurts like heck. We are torn. Rips us up inside. To think of staying and continuing makes us feel like we're dying. But the thought of leaving and divorcing overwhelms us with grief and sadness and fear. "Can't live with 'em, can't live without 'em."

Nobody can answer that question for us. It will take a lot of soul-searching and seeking good wise counsel from good wise people. You could make a list of the pros and cons. Seems a bit cold and hard, but it might reveal some insight. Talk to and listen carefully to those who are choosing to stay, as well as those who have chosen to leave. What can you learn from them?

Life will never be easy, whichever road you choose. Be careful not to fall for the fantasy that divorce removes troubles. Speaking from experience, in most cases you just exchange one set of problems for another. The bottom line: Are you or your children in danger? Are you being abused? If so, I urge you to get out. Now.

Another consideration is if you still have children at home. Unless they are in danger, it is usually in their best interest to keep mom and dad together. Divorce is devastating to children and affects them for the rest of their lives.

Get good counseling, not only for you two together, but for you alone. And hopefully for him alone too.

If you're just tired or annoyed or frustrated, I encourage you to seek a good support network and to do all you can to take really good care of yourself. Most of us who are hanging in there aren't doing so because it's easy. We do so each day because it's worth it. Learning to put ourselves at the top of our priority list is essential.

Sometimes just knowing we have the option of getting out is enough. We can feel so trapped. So stuck. So hopeless. So lifeless. But we have more power than we realize. We have the power to get up each day and choose to love. Choose to take care of ourselves. Choose to learn and grow—totally independent of what he does or doesn't do. Our choices do not require his approval or positive response.

Tom and Gina were ready to throw in the towel. The stress and drama had gone on too long. They were tired. Saw no options. Then Gina connected with some other vet wives and started getting positive encouragement. Soon Tom began getting counseling and joined a Pointman support group. They realized that faith (connection with God) and love (connection with each other and those around them) were the life-lines they so desperately needed. It has been several years now, and they have their ups and downs. But they are still together, growing and journeying together. And still glad they are.

Take inventory of yourself regularly. Sometimes we get so consumed with trying to please, placate, or avert an incident that we lose track of us. What do I need? What do I want? And that is not only okay; it is necessary!

Before throwing in the towel, take time to be sure you're doing all you can to take good care of you. Try to be more aware of how much you're trying to draw your energy and life from him instead of nourishing yourself. You don't need to be divorced to claim, "It's my turn. This is my time."

58. How can I convince him that he does not have to jump to morbid extremes and always assume the worst?

The brain affected by PTSD is constantly in survival mode. It never turns off. It never relaxes. It is always ready for an attack. Or death. Because the subconscious mind assumes that danger is always imminent, that heightened level of protection must be maintained. Along the same lines, surprises are the enemy. So if they can prepare themselves for all negative outcomes, then they feel safer. More prepared. Always plan for the worst. That way they can at least have the illusion of control. No surprises = safety.

One vet wife said that whenever she went out for her daily walk or left to do errands in the car, he assumed she would die. He always looked scared, depressed, and sad whenever she left—and oh so relieved when she actually returned alive!

Understanding how they think is always helpful. And perhaps that may be all we can do. It's not our job to convince them of anything. Remember, we can't fix them. We can love them. And encourage them. And gently remind them of reality.

They may fear the worst about themselves, about you, about your children, or everything in general. The wall they erect around themselves lends some level of feeling protected. However, it is comfortless. It is terribly lonely. And scary. When they were in the jungle or desert staring death in the face, they were so terrified they became numb. Part of the horror of it all was that they felt so terribly alone. There was no comfort. Now many years later, we can come alongside them and comfort them. Even in their fear. Especially in their fear.

When you sense him going into this mode, put your arms around him and give him a hug. Many hugs. Gentle squeezes on the hands. Back rubs. Foot massages. Kisses. Remind him how much you love him. How much you appreciate him.

When he gets frightened for your safety, reassure him by letting him

know how much you appreciate his concern for you and that you look forward to seeing him in a few hours. And it never hurts to flash him (show him some flesh!*) and make him smile. Might change his direction of thinking and bring a big smile to his face.
(*Note: Does not apply if you are his mother.)

$\mathcal{L}$♥

59. How can I make suggestions without him accusing me of controlling him?

One of the symptoms of PTSD is feeling out of control. They are driven to do all they can to stay in control. Or at least to maintain the illusion. Sometimes this results in their misinterpretation of normal words and actions of others. Their defenses shoot up and the relationship is troubled.

Paula shared with us that there hardly was a relationship between them because she had pretty much learned not to talk to him. She said, "We live a parallel existence, where you learn you can't say anything or it will be taken the wrong way." She worked hard to just keep things as pleasant as possible, but inside she was dying of sadness that she couldn't connect with her vet.

Others find that normal good-sense suggestions sometimes are rewarded with a backlash. We learn to tiptoe around our comments. And find it worth the effort. It does help to think carefully before speaking. Sometimes we women can be so enthusiastic about something and perhaps overly eager that we come across as pushy and controlling. We must slow down and remember that we are a team. We do value their input. We need their input.

Also, we can phrase things in a way to build them up, encourage them, and include them. Whatever we can do to include them in the process and the conversation, the more likely they will not have to be defensive. Include positive phrases that show appreciation for their thoughts and ideas and opinions.

Another avenue is to use questions a lot. Ask them what they think about this option or that option. You still have control over the options, but encourage them to participate. When Becky was getting ready to remodel their bathroom, she dreaded asking Bob's opinions because he was not gifted in that area. She feared he would plaster the walls with footballs and Harleys. But she was also wise enough to know not to just blast him with what she wanted and not leave room for his input. So she did a lot of research and then went out and gathered lots of samples of things she liked. That way, when she presented the options to Bob, they were all things she liked, but left plenty of room for his opinion. She laughed when he looked at one paint chip and threw it down. "No way! That green looks like the Army." The bathroom turned out great and both felt part of the process.

One more comment on this. If he or you or your kids are in danger and you need to say something, do not worry about how he may take it. Your job is to be safe. And no matter what you say, as long as you do it out of love, his response is not your responsibility.

✐

60. My vet has trouble holding down jobs. What can I do to help?

Another classic symptom of PTSD is problems in the workplace. The difficulty may be related to substance abuse, inappropriate behaviors, outbursts of rage, anxieties, resistance to authority, or any number of other behavioral or emotional issues. Some of this often results from the challenges of transitioning back into civilian life after the military. There are many excellent resources available for families of veterans in transition (see Help for Times of Transistion, page 199). However, many vets still find themselves struggling with employment issues after many years and even decades.

Not only does it cause us heartache to see our dear vets go through the ups and downs of this turmoil, it also seriously impacts us as a family in many ways. In addition to financial stress, we also have our own fears and frustrations to deal with. One disruption may be that the wife ends up carrying a heavier workload than the couple had originally anticipated.

So how do we once again love our vets and also take care of our needs? Although we can't obliterate the PTSD, we can assume a few helpful roles. The first would be as a sounding board. Can you listen and hear and support him when he needs to unload about work situations? Without jumping in with advice—at least not yet. But simply be available to listen.

Another role we can assume is cheerleader. A little encouragement goes a very long way. Be generous with our compliments and words of affirmation.

A third role is information-gatherer. There are many helpful resources available for those seeking employment and also finding the best job fit. Too often, stress in the workplace can be tied to a mismatch of job duties and natural abilities. Perhaps he can take a deeper look into his talents, abilities, and interests, and how they might line up with a more accurately matched set of job skills needed in the marketplace.

We as loved ones can do some research and offer options to our vets—things like classes, books, people to contact, or support groups. The more he can connect with others in a group and also with a good counselor, the better he'll be able to deal with his issues. Keep in mind that the PTSD carries with it tremendous anxiety about new people and places and situations. So anything you can do to offer these resources in a comfortable safe manner would be much better received.

Finally, the role of wise money manger is essential. No one likes the "B" word (budget), but it can truly make a difference. Not only for your stress but also his. I am a big fan of Dave Ramsey and his practical attainable steps to getting out of debt, taking good care of your family, and planning for retirement and future expenses.

When our vets are the man of the house, they carry a huge weight on their shoulders. They want to succeed. They want to provide. And the more we can encourage them the better, while at the same time being mindful of our needs and feelings. Just like them, we do best when we're connected to a healthy support network.

61. We are so frustrated with the official agencies that are supposed to be helping veterans. Any tips on dealing with them?

If it's any comfort, you're not alone in your sentiments. Dealing with bureaucracies is never pleasant for anyone, let alone for our valiant warriors who deserve the very best at this time in their lives. Money is tight all around and vying for it gets tougher every day. Additionally, we must consider the rapidly growing number of veterans discovering symptoms of PTSD and seeking help.

The best words of encouragement I can offer is to hang in there. Countless individuals who have shared their stories with me all appear to have one thing in common: It takes time and persistence. I've heard that people feel the VA and other agencies secretly hope you'll get so frustrated from jumping through hoops and tripping over red tape that you'll give up. Surrender. Whether that's true or not, we do know that funds are limited, and those who hang in there to the end through all the roadblocks and bumps in the road will reap the benefits of their efforts.

Alyssa and her vet are just beginning the process of getting help, not only mental health support but also financial compensation. Intending to encourage her, Denise shared that she and her vet had just received their compensation. It only took them eight years!

There are a few things that might help expedite the process. First, be sure all your papers are in order. This was one of the problems for Denise and her vet. However, due to her relentless persistence, involving laborious research into old library records (among other things), she was able to follow a trail of information that eventually led to the appropriate documentation required. Barbara's Vietnam vet was denied for many years because the VA couldn't find any record that he ever served. (The shrapnel in his head and his missing arm did not convince them.) Thankfully, after much persistence she was able to dig up the old faded document that they needed.

Keep accurate and detailed records of all your conversations and interactions with the bureaucracy personnel. Don't let a "no" answer stop you. If you can enlist a case manager who is on the ball, someone who can coordinate your efforts, stay in constant communication with that person and be sure to express your appreciation.

One vet was particularly overwhelmed and discouraged in his quest for help that included both evaluation and compensation. Thankfully, he was blessed to have a fellow veteran who stood beside him the whole way and encouraged him. His information and insights from his own experience proved to be very helpful. Five years later, as this vet was preparing to go in for his final evaluation, he panicked and began to retreat. Thankfully, his buddy stood right there with him and prayed for him in the lobby of this government building. Imagine! Thirty minutes later, he came back out with his total and permanent status. Many others will testify that seeking God in the entire process is the best way to go.

Another thing to consider is researching as many organizations as you can that exist to help veterans. As the need continues to grow, so do the attempts to meet them. Check online for organizations that may be of help.

Finally, stay connected to other veterans and their families. We have found that networking is truly a treasure! Ask around and keep your ears open. We all can benefit from each other, especially in this area.

62. He loves things that involve risk (guns, motorcycles, etc.) that worry me. Is it my place to stop him from doing recreational things that are dangerous, or do I just stuff my concerns?

One vet was almost killed three different times on his motorcycle (three different motorcycles). By the third time, his wife, Linda, understandably did not want him to get another. First she just requested it. He had no intention of stopping his riding. He said it made him feel alive and free and he could not envision living without it. Then she expressed all kinds of thoughts to force him not to get one (bribes, threats, etc.), which did not go over well. They were definitely at odds and unable to arrive at a mutual decision.

Eventually, Linda faced her fears. Let her guard down. Felt and owned her fear. She expressed to him that she was so afraid he would die. When she approached him in tenderness and vulnerability, both of their walls came down. At that point they were able to at least discuss it further rather than fighting about it (which gets us nowhere). It made him feel good to know she loved him, and that her fear was a result of love rather than a control issue. That also helped his guard come down.

When walls are up, there is no communication, no connection, and no hope for resolve. At that point they agreed to put it on hold for the time being. It's a really good thing to be able to discuss issues. Often decisions require time. They are a process. Sometimes you just need to agree to revisit the issue again soon, not stuffing it and not rushing into it. Instead, process it together in multiple conversations.

Over time, she realized two things. First, they could make a compromise. He would get a dirt bike instead of a street bike, thereby lessening the risk. She also realized that if he still insisted on getting another street bike, she would have to let go. Scary, but necessary. She realized that in wanting the best for him (including life), that meant that he needed his freedom to take risks. That was life for him. He would likely shrivel up inside if he couldn't do the thing he loved so much. So she lives with that fear and comforts herself by remembering that she would rather he lived and loved his life while he can. Otherwise, he would become a prisoner, slowly dying inside from resentment.

Many of our vets love guns. Also a tremendous risk. But it's not up to us to control our vets out of fear. If they're taking the necessary safety precautions, then we need to just let go. Like Linda, we need to first own our fears and other feelings, express them in love, and then let go. If there are creative alternatives and other options that might be safer, we can certainly present them. But ultimately, we want our vets to live their lives to the fullest while they can. And always remind them how much we love them.

ℒ♥

63. I'm in a relationship with my vet who has PTSD. We're not married (yet). I'm sort of afraid to commit. But I really love him. How do I know whether or not to stick with him? Are there any signs that would show me that he's worth the risk of a lifelong commitment?

I admire your wisdom in asking these questions. This is indeed the time to take a candid look at the relationship using both right brain (feelings/emotions) and left brain (logic/facts). It's easy to just say, "I love him," and then hope that will be enough to take care of all the reality ahead. Unfortunately, we all know that's not enough. Everybody longs for a happy, healthy, and fulfilling relationship. But sometimes you have to wait for it. If he's not the right person for you, please do not try to make him become that dream man. It does not work. He is who he is, and this may not be a match for you.

When I was considering marrying my vet, I took classes and read all I could on PTSD. I also had individual counseling and we had couples' counseling, both with professionals who were experienced with PTSD issues. One thing that stood out in my mind was the concept that they are "wounded soldiers." If you love your man and he's a wounded soldier because of his PTSD, that does not in itself prevent a fulfilling marriage. And on the flip side, just because he's a wounded soldier does not automatically qualify him to be a wonderful husband. The PTSD will always affect both of you, but it does not provide a license for bad behavior.

I wish I could give you a nice formula with ten little questions to ask yourself and a nice neat score to determine your future. But instead I will give you some things to think about as you ponder this huge decision. I see three things to use as guides in your decision process:

1. How is his relationship with God?
2. How is his relationship with you?
3. How is his relationship with himself and others?

A man who has faith, a connection with God, will be a man to share your life with. Not perfect. Not outwardly "religious." But growing and genuine. Do you see this in him? Do you see him progressing (at any rate) on his spiritual journey?

A man who loves you unconditionally and shows it is a man to share your life with. That connection is a key to holding your relationship together in those dark and lonely cave days. And brings him back when he gets triggered. How does he show his love for you?

A man who takes care of himself, consistently makes healthy choices, and is kind to other people, is a man to share your life with. What good things does he do for his health and well being? And how does he treat others?

These are all positive keys to a fulfilling committed relationship. Now for some huge red flags. If you see any of these, my advice would be to get out now:

1. Does he abuse alcohol or drugs?
2. Does he abuse you verbally or physically?
3. Is he unwilling to learn and grow and take the steps he needs in order to be healthy?

Just in the last few months four ladies came to me. Two had been married for many years, and two were living with their vets and considering marriage. All four were in similar situations. He drank too much. He used drugs. He was mean. And he beat her up often. She was scared and wanted to get out, but felt trapped because she was financially dependent on him. She also felt guilty and wanted to stay because she still loved him. She hoped he would change. Each day was up and down as she monitored his behavior. Life was a frightening and exhausting roller coaster. She was encouraged to get a restraining order to protect her life.

I still remember hearing them say,

"I know he is a good man on the inside." (Really? And he beats up your face and throws you against the wall?)

"He has PTSD. If we work hard enough it can be fixed." (Really? PTSD is not responsible for these behaviors. Nice try.)

"I can't abandon him now. He needs me." (Really? He needs you so he can beat on someone?)

"I still love him." (Really? Sure doesn't appear to help much.)

"He has so many good qualities." (Really? When he's choking you, does it matter that he's nice to the mailman or that he takes out the garbage?)

"I wish it was like it used to be when we first fell in love." (And you're holding out because you think you can change him?)

And the winner is: "Four days every week he is either drunk or leaves without telling me where he is, but the other three days he is good." (Really? And this is life you are choosing?)

Sad to say, only one of those four women's situations worked out. And it was because he took responsibility for his actions and he made changes. As she saw that he was serious and committed to a healthy relationship, things got better.

If he is hurting you or your children in *any way*, get out. If he is abusing substances in any way, get out. If he shows no signs of changing and working on his issues, get out. The good news is that if he sees you are serious and you draw the line, he might change.

I encourage you to get counseling together in addition to individual counseling. Be sure to find a counselor who is up on PTSD. If you decide to give him a "probation" period, spell out specifically what he needs to do and in what time frame. For instance, "If we are to proceed with this relationship, I need to see the following three things in the next six months: 1. You attend Alcoholics Anonymous daily for six months and stop drinking; 2. You do not touch me hurtfully at all for six months; 3. You go to your VA counselor regularly every week for the next six months." (Or whatever you need to see in him, and however much time it requires for you to be sure.) Better to take a long time than too short a time. Some people may even want to make it two or three years, depending on the situation.

Sarah was in love with her vet, Brent, and about to get engaged. But she'd noticed over time that he really had a problem with anger, among other things. It was the road rage that concerned her most. He was putting her in danger. Unfortunately (or fortunately), it took an accident to give her a wake-up call.

She was healthy enough to draw a line. This was it. She told him to either get help or she was history. Not without a lot of agony on her part, but at least it was the right thing to do. Had he blown her off, leaving would have definitely been the right thing to do. But bless his heart, he took it seriously himself.

The next day Brent went to the vet center and began counseling. He is taking an anger management class and going to a group now. He owns his problem and is openly talking about his PTSD with Sarah now. She said that for the first time she sees he has hope. Wow! Good job, Sarah and Brent. It is not a fix-all, but they are making good choices, getting help, and going in the right direction. She said that even his driving has improved.

One more thing: If you have drawn a line and are going through a "probation" period, it will be most effective if you don't have sex with him. (Bummer, huh?) But even that will keep things moving in the right direction. Then if he does make life-altering genuine changes, you'll be able to celebrate for the rest of your lives! And if he chooses to go downhill further, then you won't regret giving him access to your body anymore.

Learn all you can about PTSD and seek wisdom and counsel from those around you and those who know him. And take your time. If you listen to wisdom, you will know.

✒

64. Can I Get Triggered Too?

It is easy to forget that living with our vets' PTSD can affect us too. But it does, and just when we think we have it all together.

One typical morning I was in "go" mode, on my way out for the day.

We had our prayer and hug at the back door, and I trotted down the driveway to the car. As soon as I put the car in gear, BOOM! What was that? I broke the car! The engine fell out! It's gonna blow up! We can't afford a new car! Freaked out, panicked, and triggered, I ran back up to the house. When my husband saw my panic, it triggered him, too.

We darted down the driveway, fully activated. He got in the car and turned it on. Pulled it forward. Turned it off. Wow. I was speechless. (I did manage to sneak in a prayer along the way. Always a good thing.) Then he got out, handed me the keys, and smiled. I learned three things that day. First, my husband is wonderful (I already knew that). Second, I can get triggered too. And third, cars go much better when you *take off* the parking brake. (Good, Welby.) It was humbling in many ways. And now I know I *too* am susceptible to triggers. I was reminded that panicking is not always productive.

So why do we go from small problem to global disaster in two seconds? One word: PTSD. They have it. And so do we, at some level.

Our loved ones' PTSD affects us more than we realize. The most important thing is to first be aware. When we start to panic, or get triggered in any way, can we pause long enough to recognize it? Sometimes that will be enough in and of itself. We cannot instantly fix our feelings or reactions, but we can gradually become more mindful of them. By doing this, we get a little stronger and a little more stable.

We need help both during, and between episodes. Remember that PTSD results from exposure to a life-threatening trauma (or one that is perceived as a threat). During this trauma, the body instantly kicks into survival mode. Because the trauma was so severe and because our bodies are hardwired for survival, the trauma is permanently programmed into us, resulting in PTSD. From then on every reminder of that initial trauma, internal or external, is a potential trigger. When triggered, or reactivated, we almost literally go back into the heat of the battle and relive the trauma. The hardwiring that preserved our lives in battle become an enemy in and of itself.

Some triggers might be specific sounds, smells, temperature changes, sights, feelings, memories, thoughts, emotions, scenes...*anything* that reminds our programmed bodies of the trauma. Instantly we are launched into crisis survival mode! And the hardest part is that they usually come unannounced. No warning. And that is when we react.

Remember that the trauma catapults us into freeze, fight, or flight. Although the PTSD makes us feel helpless, we are not. The following are some reminders I use that have proven beneficial when I'm triggered:

1. Don't freeze; BREATHE slowly and deeply.
2. Don't fight; SPEAK calmly, "I feel ____," and "I need ____."
3. Don't run; THINK about what your body needs now to make it feel safe.

BOTTOM LINE: Don't let the panic escalate. At the first sign of reaction, do something physical (breathe, sing, walk, pray out loud, drink water, hug your dog or loved one, count backward, etc.).

AFTER CALMING DOWN:

DON'T waste energy resenting the PTSD; try to ACCEPT it and go forward.

DON'T let your identity get lost; stay ALIVE and grounded.

DON'T try to do it alone; CONNECT with others for support.

DON'T minimize the importance of your own issues; continue to get good COUNSELING.

DON'T let their PTSD and yours pool together; DIFFERENTIATE their triggers from yours.

DON'T sweep it all under the rug and hope it goes away; TALK together about their triggers and yours.

DON'T play the victim; take preemptive CONTROL to avoid triggers.

DON'T be passive; have a clear, simple PLAN in place.

DON'T forget about triggers during the good times; stay TUNED to the first warning signs.

DON'T beat yourself up for not being perfect; keep on LEARNING and be willing to grow.

And the best for last: DON'T put life on hold; ENJOY the good days to the fullest!

Our vets' PTSD does indeed affect all of us. We *will* get triggered. As challenging as it may be, it does not have to prevent us from loving and fully living. And I am finding that the more we can laugh at ourselves, the more our sense of humor also has the opportunity to grow!

PART TWO

REPLENISH

Our Needs

Congratulations! You're doing just what you need right now: taking care of you!! We who expend so much love and energy on our vets, in addition to all the other demands of life, are often on the verge of collapse. Teetering precariously on the edge of the cliff and just trying to hang on for dear life. One mother of a vet referred to PTSD as a "soul-stealing illness," both for our vets and for those of us who love them. Now it's time to take care of us. Replenish.

So much energy is continually going out of us. Work, children, our spouse, aging parents, friends, shopping, repairs, laundry, medical issues, text messages, and all the other things that scream relentlessly at us all day long. It seems like the whole world demands our attention. We are tired. We are depleted. Exhausted. Burned out. Yet we cannot afford the luxury of slowing down. Taking care of us is a foreign concept, and definitely not allowed—or so we have assumed.

One thing I'm trying to remember is that most of us are by nature givers. The fact that we have been drawn to our vets is evidence that we love to give. We love to nurture and help. Yet sometimes we find ourselves depleted. No surprise. Sometimes we assume we are infinite, with an endless supply of love and energy. Unfortunately, it takes illness, meltdowns, or complete exhaustion to give us a wake-up call. We are finite. We are human. And that is okay! A little humbling for those of us who like to fix the world and everyone in it.

But it is also freeing to realize not only that we *cannot* do everything, we don't *have* to. Yay!

We get so busy doing that we forget to pause and take inventory of ourselves. When was the last time you asked yourself, "What do I need?" It takes conscious effort to remember to take care of ourselves. We need to nurture ourselves and be sure to replenish with good healthy things. Take in what is good for us. Soak it up!

WE ARE GOOD TO THOSE AROUND US…
BE GOOD TO OURSELVES TOO!

The following is a list of twenty-one common needs. Rather than lecture you about them (if you want a lecture you can read other books, research on the internet, or call your mother), I have framed it in a survey format. This will help you think through each need and hopefully clarify what is lacking and what specifically needs to be replenished. I encourage you to share this with someone else who can cheer you on as you endeavor to do the very best for you.

1. Breathe.

We get so focused on what we're doing or where we're going that we can forget to breathe! Fresh air and deep breaths can be cleansing, energizing, and calming. Count in to five. And count out slowly again for five counts. Take in good happy thoughts as you inhale.

_____ I hardly get outside much anymore.

_____ I smoke like a chimney, but I plan to quit tomorrow.

_____ I use synthetic chemical "air fresheners" in my home and car to try to cover up stinky smells. I use laundry products with artificial fragrance.

_____ Car fumes and yard equipment poison my fresh air too often.

_____ I notice that sometimes I hold my breath when I'm stressed.

_____ When I'm driving or tense about something, my breathing is short and quick and shallow.

_____ Breathing in and out slowly helps me relax.

_____ I do what I can to avoid toxic fumes.

_____ We have a good air filtration system in our home.

_____ I love to go outside and get a breath of refreshing air whenever I get a chance.

_____ My dog has taught me the thrill of sticking my head out the car window and letting my ears flap in the fresh air.

_____ When I find myself feeling anxious, I pause and take three very slow deep breaths from my abdomen not my shoulders.

2. Soak up all the love you receive.

Sometimes we get so busy giving love to others that we forget to take it in for ourselves. Enjoy every bit of love that comes your way. Open up your heart and let it flow in.

_____ I tend to give a lot to others.

_____ Sometimes I don't feel worthy of being loved.

____ When someone gives me a compliment, I sort of brush it off.

____ When I receive an encouraging email or note in the mail, I just read it and go on with my day.

____ I'm often in a hurry and don't hold still long enough to receive a long hug.

____ Bah. Humbug.

____ I feel I should give a lot more and receive less.

____ I cherish all words of affection I get.

____ I put my cards up on my desk or the mantle and enjoy them.

____ I'm blessed to be surrounded by loving people.

____ My dog really loves me, and the cat tries his best to let me think he doesn't care, but I soak up all their furry affection.

____ When someone tells me they love me, it feels so good.

____ I know I'm lovable in spite of my imperfections.

____ I love how good it feels to get a hug.

3.   Seek out wise counsel.

We cannot do this alone. There are many resources, both people and materials, that can guide us along in wisdom. The more we reach out and receive that guidance the smoother our path will be.

____ Throughout my life I have listened to bad advice.

____ I like radio talk shows and TV shows where people are constantly at each other; the drama is entertaining.

____ I don't know where to go when I feel angry, overwhelmed, or stuck.

____ I am pretty self-sufficient and do not need others' advice.

____ Bart Simpson is my hero.

____ Counselors are for people who are weak or mentally ill.

_____ I don't have time to read.

_____ I have a good counselor I can go to anytime.

_____ When I have spiritual questions, I seek out my pastor, minister, priest, rabbi, mentor, or other spiritual leader.

_____ I know I can't do this on my own; I need help.

_____ I love connecting with a group of others in the same situation.

_____ I'm open to learning.

_____ It encourages me to pick up a new resource that will be helpful to me in my struggles.

_____ I'm reading this book.

4. Surround yourself with healthy people who are good for you.

We need all the good vibes we can get. Healthy people will build us up. Unhealthy people drain us of our good energy and will eventually suck us dry. We get to choose who we spend our time with.

_____ My family and friends are always giving me their not-so-good opinions.

_____ I feel drained when I've been with my friends.

_____ It seems like the people I hang out with are always putting others down.

_____ I am drawn to needy individuals.

_____ My friends are all very photogenic. Just look at their mug shots.

_____ We never seem to do anything beneficial except indulge.

_____ My friends and I share the same values.

_____ My friends are interested in hearing about things I'm learning and how I'm growing.

_____ I feel safe around them and can trust them.

_____ I look forward to being with them.

_____ Sometimes we laugh so hard the milk comes out our noses.

_____ My friends are a good source of encouragement to me.

5.   Create a special safe place that is just for you.

There will be times when you need to get all alone, whether to be safe or just to recharge. Use your creativity to make a cozy hideaway just for you. A special place that you love, that you find soothing, comforting, and pleasant.

_____ I don't have any place I can get away to when I feel scared.

_____ I feel so drained and in need of a place to rest.

_____ I never know where to go when I feel like running away.

_____ I wish I had a quiet place to just sit and think.

_____ You telling me I need a vacation?!

_____ Sometimes I feel like I've lost myself and can't find me.

_____ I don't know what I would do without my little corner downstairs.

_____ I can flop down in an old cushy chair with a cozy blanket and pillows in my favorite colors.

_____ My alone time is precious.

_____ I love to curl up with a good book and my favorite music.

_____ A nice beach in Hawaii sounds good.

_____ When I rejoin the world after being in my special place, I feel recharged.

6.   Take a regular physical inventory of your body.

It's important to continually do a body scan in order to keep unwanted emotions from sabotaging us. Listen to what your body is trying to tell you. Sometimes it helps to ask, "Am I tired, hungry, or hormonal?"

_____ I get uptight often.

_____ At times I just blow up without warning.

_____ I have stomach troubles and headaches.

_____ I get really cranky if I haven't eaten.

_____ I'm so focused on taking care of everybody else that I forget to tune in to what I need until it's too late.

_____ Hand over the chocolate and nobody will get hurt.

_____ When my shoulders start to get tense, I stop and ask myself what's bothering me.

_____ I've learned to be especially aware of my body and emotions right before my period.

_____ Sometimes I find myself hunched over forward with stress, so I remind myself to stand up straight and do the exercise, "We must, we must, we must develop our bust!"

_____ When I start to get irritable, I stop and ask myself if I'm short on sleep.

_____ I notice that when I clench my jaw, that usually means I have some stuff to work through.

_____ I'm more aware of my growing hunger before I get too hungry, so I can eat better and sooner.

7.   **Saturate every sense with good and pleasant things.**

Seeing, hearing, smelling, tasting, and touching can all be filled with things that are pleasant and good for us. The more we fill all our senses with good and pleasurable things, the healthier and happier we will be.

_____ I don't enjoy healthy food.

_____ I'm long overdue for a massage.

_____ It's been a long time since I smelled a rose.

_____ I spend most of my time inside and rarely stop to enjoy a beautiful tree or sunset.

_____ I find great pleasure in cheesecake, donuts, and large fries.

____ My life is so noisy. I need some soothing music.

____ I love savoring my food instead of scarfing it down.

____ The highlight of my day is to soak in a lavender bubble bath with vanilla candles.

____ Whenever I feel tired, I ask my husband to give me a back rub.

____ Speaking of husband, do orgasms count?

____ My collection of favorite CDs is growing.

____ I'm amazed at the intricate beauty of one tiny flower.

8. Practice healthy boundaries.

There are times when we need to place a priority on our needs—even at the risk of displeasing another person. Using our wisdom and staying tuned to what we need helps us know when that time is and how to do it as graciously as possible.

____ I'm a people pleaser.

____ It's hard for me to say "No."

____ I often feel resentful that people are taking advantage of me.

____ Sometimes I get sick from doing too much for others and not listening to my own body.

____ Maybe I could get a tattoo on my forehead that says, "Just say No!"

____ I wish at times that I could have more time and space for me, but then I feel guilty.

____ I don't have to do everything everybody wants me to do.

____ It is possible to say, "No, I'm unable to do that, but thanks for asking."

_____ When someone speaks to me or treats me inappropriately, I can say, "That is not acceptable."

_____ I don't need to give reasons to people or defend myself when I decline a plea or invitation.

_____ Telemarketers and solicitors hate me.

_____ I feel better when I can take care of my needs, and then when all is said and done, I have more energy to spend on others.

9. Get plenty of sleep.

In our always-on-the-go culture, sleep can be considered a luxury, not a necessity. Until you don't get enough. Which is way too often. We desperately need plenty of sleep in order to function well both emotionally and physically.

_____ I pride myself on how little sleep I get.

_____ It's not the quantity but the quality that counts; I can get by with little.

_____ I'm too busy to get all the sleep I really need.

_____ I'd feel really guilty if I ever took a nap.

_____ I could never go out in public with those little pillow wrinkle lines on my face.

_____ I wish I had more energy.

_____ I feel good and rested when I get up in the morning.

_____ I allow myself time for naps whenever I can.

_____ There's a lot to be said for snoring and drooling (not sure what!).

_____ Sometimes I need more sleep than usual, and I make an effort to get more sleep at those times.

_____ I'm not embarrassed by getting adequate sleep.

_____ I do what I can to have good quality sleep (use earplugs, sleep machine, good mattress, etc.).

10.   Remember to take care of your medical needs too.

Taking care of other family members and loved ones can take its toll on our health—and all too often without us realizing it. We are not immortal or beyond having our own unique health needs. Let's not forget to put ourselves at the top of the list in this area.

_____ I feel pretty good and will wait for problems before I go get a checkup.

_____ My doctor wants me to take some pills, but it's such a hassle. I probably don't need them anyway.

_____ My blood pressure is probably pretty good; I think around 360 or so.

_____ I've always had good health, so I should be fine.

_____ His medical concerns are so much more urgent than mine.

_____ I know there's a concern and I'll give it my attention when I have more time.

_____ I always schedule my annual exams (gotta love those stirrups).

_____ If I notice anything that concerns me, I make an appointment with the doctor.

_____ I realize the value and importance of taking my meds and supplements regularly.

_____ I'm committed to following through with what the doctor recommends for me.

_____ The sound of my dentist's drill is music to my ears, especially when it's coming from the other chair.

_____ I know I need to be in good health in order to best care for my loved ones.

11.   Eat and drink for good health.

Our cells are designed to thrive when they're properly nourished and to get sick and die when they're not. We're so fortunate to be able to have such an abundance of healthy nourishing foods available to us. We know what they are. Now we just have to choose to do it. And we will never regret the payoff!

____ I eat on the run.

____ Cooking and food prep takes too much time.

____ I love lots of starchy and fatty foods.

____ What does the word "organic" mean?

____ I shouldn't eat sweets, but I do. Love that sugar.

____ I eat and drink a lot of diet foods with artificial sweetener that I know is probably not good for me.

____ Water?

____ I sneak my kids' gummy vitamins when they're not looking.

____ After I got off sugar, everything started tasting so good! And my cravings for it stopped.

____ Vegetables are not punishment for being evil.

____ When I eat food rich in nutrients, I'm satisfied and don't binge eat.

____ Do I have to eat fish? (I cheat and take fish oil capsules.)

____ I never realized how good our filtered water was until I went to a restaurant and they served swimming pool water.

____ Wow. I feel good!

12. Express your needs.

The more we let our needs and desires be known, the better we do. Taking care of ourselves requires that occasionally we have to ask for something. This is healthy and freeing. And also helpful to those around us.

____ Others should be able to read my mind.

_____ My needs are the same as everyone else's, so I don't need to verbalize them.

_____ If I ask for something when he's in a bad mood, it will just make things worse.

_____ I want what I want and I want it *now*. No exceptions.

_____ What I really need is a European vacation and a brand new Ferrari (pink, please).

_____ Asking for what I need is self-centered and not loving.

_____ I don't know how to word it right so it's easier to be quiet.

_____ I can't expect to get what I need if I don't let them know.

_____ They don't have to always be jumping up and down with joy at what I request.

_____ I realize that my requests may not always be granted and I can deal with that.

_____ It feels really good to have the freedom and strength that comes with expressing my needs and desires graciously.

_____ I have to know what I need before I can express it.

_____ I really, really need some ice cream (chocolate chip cookie dough with hot fudge on top please!).

_____ I promised my husband that he'd never have to wonder or try to guess what I needed.

13. Embrace growth.

If we ever stop learning and growing, then we might as well stop living. Life is tough. Everyone has challenges. It's up to us whether we will just endure them or become better because of them.

_____ I do all I can to control my circumstances so life goes easier.

_____ I think I'm better than most people; they are the ones who need to change.

_____ After a hard episode, I just focus ahead without examining what I could learn from it.

_____ The best strategy is to hurry through the hard times to get comfortable again.

_____ My life sucks. I plan to win the lottery so I will have no more problems.

_____ In spite of how uncomfortable it is, I try to look at my behavior and see how I might do things differently in the future.

_____ I like to look back at my life and see how much I've grown already, which makes it easier to know I will survive more growth.

_____ My husband could testify that I still have plenty of growing room left.

_____ It feels good to move forward and become stronger.

_____ I cannot change the world around me, but I can change me.

_____ I like who I'm becoming.

14. Meditate on scriptures or other uplifting wisdom.

The love and energy we pour out is further energized by spiritual wisdom. The more we can fill our minds with uplifting words, the more practical guidance and personal peace we will enjoy.

_____ I barely have time to eat my toast let alone meditate.

_____ It's too hard to pick a good source of spiritual wisdom.

_____ My mind is full already.

_____ I grew up with that stuff and it didn't do any good.

_____ I have a lot of wisdom already and probably could write one of those books myself.

_____ There's something unexplainably empowering about scriptures.

_____ I find I do best on the days when I have that in my mind and heart.

_____ The more I live and the older I get, the more I see the real necessity for and wisdom of these words.

_____ I'm such a distractible wiggle worm I can't sit still, but I can do my meditating on walks and in the car.

_____ My perspective improves so much when I've been thinking about spiritual truths.

15.   Exercise regularly in a way that you enjoy!

We all know the tremendous benefits of exercise, and we know how good we feel when we do. The key is to choose an activity that is fun rather than stressful. The payoff is well worth it!

_____ I'm not really very fat. It's just that the dryer shrunk all my clothes.

_____ I hate aerobics.

_____ As soon as I lose some weight and look better, I'll start exercising.

_____ My job is to make sure no one steals the sofa (so far so good).

_____ Running hurts my joints.

_____ I only exercise as punishment for eating too much.

_____ I usually don't feel like exercising at first but sure feel great after!

_____ I don't crave bad food as much when I exercise well.

_____ If I feel fat, I'm less inclined to do it; but if I envision myself as fit, then it goes much better.

_____ The older I get the more I jiggle, and that doesn't frighten me anymore because I know it's healthy jiggling.

_____ I love my walks!

_____ I can handle the day so much better when I've had a good workout.

16.   Revive the joy in your life: laugh and play.

You mean it's okay to have fun? We were born wanting to play all the time and there's no reason we still can't. It's up to us to not allow the burdens and stresses of life to weigh us down and obliterate our happy selves.

_____ My job and duties at home are not funny.

_____ Laughter is a luxury.

_____ A few beers will get me going.

_____ My husband and kids are always goofing off and it's my job to keep them on task.

_____ What do you mean "play"?

_____ Life's too short to have fun.

_____ As long as I can laugh at myself, I'll always have a source of humor.

_____ When I deviate from my routine a bit and try something fun, it is surprisingly enjoyable.

_____ I want to laugh so hard my stomach hurts (good way to tone the abs!).

_____ My family and friends have such a good time when I lighten up a bit.

_____ Life's too short to be serious all the time.

17.   Take time to relax and slow down.

Ever feel like life is a whirlwind? Or a treadmill that never stops? Our culture is madly driven. And it gets crazier by the minute. It takes conscious effort on our part to deliberately slow down and take the time we desperately need to refresh and renew our bodies and minds.

_____ My phone and computer are way too slow.

_____ It never fails. I always hit the red lights in traffic and get in the wrong line at the grocery store.

_____ My days off are more hectic than the days I work.

_____ I rarely get a vacation, and when I do we are on the go.

_____ I feel guilty if I'm not busy.

_____ Only sluggards waste time by relaxing.

_____ I never turn off my cell phone.

_____ I feel so much better after a power nap. Or even a long one.

_____ I try to block out some time each day to pause.

_____ My counselor told me to go home and learn to waste a little time.

_____ When I write "put feet up for 20 minutes" on my to-do list, I feel like I've accomplished something when I check it off as done. And I have!

_____ I love being a turtle rather than a hare (hope I don't look like one!).

_____ People may not like it when I turn off my phone and don't jump at each text message.

_____ I love my blob days (aka bathrobe days).

18. Let go.

What are those things that are beyond our control that we need to let go of? Expectations, resentment, imperfections? Holding out for a perfect life with perfect people will reward us with frustration and disappointment. The choice is ours whether or not we forgive, release unrealistic expectations, and leave the rest up to God.

_____ What was done to me is unforgivable.

_____ I get really ticked off when others don't do what they're supposed to do.

_____ I can usually manipulate things to go my way.

_____ Only stupid people forgive.

_____ I believe in justice, and I refuse to quit until they've paid for what they did.

_____ I try to remember that I'm not responsible for what is beyond my control (which is pretty much everything!).

_____ Forgiveness is not saying that what they did was okay, but it is letting go of my perceived responsibility to repay or punish them for it.

_____ Forgiveness is mostly about not letting it eat me up inside (physically and emotionally).

_____ Of course I'm grateful for all the forgiveness I have received.

_____ I love not having to run the universe anymore. (I used to help out but got fired.)

19.   Count your blessings.

Whether the glass is half full or half empty is up to us. Every morning we awaken to another chance at life. Our blessings are abundant, if only we will choose to see them.

_____ There's always some sort of hassle no matter what.

_____ People are unreliable.

_____ I wish there wasn't so much fattening food around to tempt me.

_____ This body is getting older and weaker and hurts more.

_____ The economy really gets me down.

_____ The future looks pretty bleak.

_____ Oh great. I have a gigantic zit on my nose.

_____ Even if the sun doesn't come out, I'm glad it's still there.

_____ Many people in the world would give anything to be fat.

_____ What a joy to be able to love and be loved.

_____ I'm grateful for ears to hear and eyes to see the beauty
around me.

_____ Having a roof over my head is a blessing.

_____ I hope I never adopt an entitlement mentality, feeling like
I deserve to have everything I want.

_____ At least I have eyes to see the zit.

20.   Feed your spiritual life.

The more we grow in our relationship with God, the more we have for
ourselves and the more we have to give. So much of burnout and deple-
tion results from trying to do life in our own strength. The well eventually
dries up. Where can you get the inner strength and source of love that
can continue to refill? What a blessing not only to us but to those around
us when we can overflow.

_____ I feel spiritually dry.

_____ I can only give so much before I burn out.

_____ People expect me to be kind and loving and patient and
giving, but I need all that too.

_____ Some days I want to resign.

_____ I wish I had a source of energy and goodness like a spring
that was always available.

_____ I wish I were closer to God.

_____ I do better when I lean on my Higher Power.

_____ It's good to know I can always come to Him for help.

_____ The more I get fed, the more I have to give.

_____ I'm like a car with a gas tank that needs to be filled regularly or I'll end up on the side of the road...just my luck
to not have a gas can.

_____ The precursor to being filled is to recognize that I'm empty.

_____ He has never let me down.

21.   Pursue your life purpose.

We are not here by chance. Haphazard as it may seem at times, each life has a purpose. It is our privilege and responsibility to pursue that unique purpose and in doing so to find fulfillment for ourselves and blessing for those around us.

_____ I don't have any special talents.

_____ I haven't set any goals except to just make it through each day.

_____ Fulfillment is a luxury for the lucky.

_____ I'm good at eating and sleeping and very talented at using the remote.

_____ My piano teacher requested that I not return for any more lessons.

_____ There are many things I love to do, and I just need to develop them more.

_____ I recognize that I'm weak in some areas and strong in others.

_____ I still can't keep the crayons inside the lines, but boy am I finally good at writing.

_____ The more I use my gifts and abilities, the better I get and the more I enjoy them!

_____ It helps me get through each day knowing that nothing is wasted; everything is part of a plan.

PTSD FAMILY SUPPORT, LLC

PART THREE

REFLECT

Our Wisdom

The following is a collection of heart-baring wisdom gleaned from the real lives of many, including me, who love our vets. I am truly grateful for the precious people God has put along my pathway. Thank you to everyone who lives the day-to-day reality of loving our vets and who encourages the rest of us to do the same.

❧

If I had known before what I know now about PTSD, I probably would not have gone forward with the relationship. But now that I'm here, I'm committed to making it the best it can be. And being the best I can be.

❧

We do not always need an instant solution.

❧

I have been *with* him instead of trying to *fix* him. I have noticed a huge improvement!

❧

My frustration and anger is not at him, but at his trauma and abuse.

❧

My vet's experiences are the most painful and violent of all that I've heard or read. I have always felt bad, like I was the only one, for not wanting to hear his stories. They are so horrendous! It has just been the last year that he has had flashbacks and all this stuff is coming out. And he wants to talk to me about it. I hate it! The more I hear the further down it takes me. I get depressed, angry, anxious, sleepless, and everything else that he is feeling comes inside me too. They say we need to listen to them, but I got to the point where I didn't think I could do it anymore. And I was a bad wife.

After talking to others who have been at this much longer, I'm realizing that my feelings are normal. I'm not bad, but I need to pay attention to my own alarms inside of me. I can listen to him without letting the unspeakable stuff suck me into a deep dark hole. What I'm learning to do is sit with him, hold his hand or put my arm around him, and just let him pour it all out. Rather than letting myself become him and taking on his entire trauma, I visualize it going right past me instead of inside of me. I have a mental file box that it goes into.

It doesn't help him for me to parallel his PTSD. And that only makes me sicker. But it helps us both when he can process his stuff, and I can be with him as he does. It has taken me awhile to get the hang of it. But it is getting so much better.

***

For years and years, things were so bad. At that time no one was talking about PTSD. Neither of us had ever even heard of it. I didn't understand he had problems with PTSD until we were married for twenty-five years. Then he went and got help. He was so relieved; he shouted, "I am not crazy!" Then I went to four rounds of classes to learn more about PTSD. I read all I could. It all made sense. I had a lot of anger in me and I knew something was wrong.

Over the years, it was real hard for me and my kids to try to understand what was going on. He was so moody. He buried himself in his work and struggled with drugs. To get numb. One thing that I did was I tried to create a normal family life. I came from a very close family. We had family gatherings and the camaraderie. I worked hard to provide that for us. He really craved that. It was important to him that my family accepted him and was willing to listen to him when others would not. I really appreciate my friends who stood up for us. That meant a lot.

Looking back, knowing what I do now, to be honest the first thing I wish I had done differently was run! But because I cared so much for him I have stayed. It's such a complex disability. They're just now starting to realize the depth. I see so many common traits in these guys. And we as wives all look shell-shocked, as if we had been through the war ourselves. I want a spa day!

What I have done to take care of me is try to avoid any confrontation. I try to keep everything really calm. But I lost myself and stuffed my emotions. I stuffed myself with food. I lost my self-esteem. I'm just trying now to do that differently. Learning to eat better and to recognize the feelings as they come before I stuff them back down with food.

Another really huge thing I've learned is that you gotta have faith. The only thing that has pulled me through is that I have to lean on God. He is in charge of this. I truly question whether I am strong enough. I could not do it without Him. The spiritual aspect is the key. I'm giving it over to God or my Higher Power. I get a sense of peace because He is so much bigger than we are.

I remember asking the counselor if there is a cure for PTSD. I don't think you ever get over it; you just learn to manage it. Once someone has been through experiences like they have, it's life-changing. Can't change them, but you can get help. I wish I had gotten help and understanding earlier on. It's so much better if you can break the cycles and patterns earlier on and adjust or reset things, rather than have it ingrained in you. Patience Mason's book really hit home. I want to know what we are dealing with and why. There is so much more information out there than there ever was. I wish he could have gotten the help earlier. It is so ingrained in him I don't know if he will ever get well. But at least understanding gives him more peace. You are not alone. And the "Oh yeah" moments.

I find out every day how big an issue this is. There are no simple answers. There is no magic pill.

Advice I would offer is learn to focus on yourself. Don't give everything, because you are not helping them. If you don't have anything left, you're in trouble. Even though you think "I'll just give more; then it will be okay. " Then you have two toxic people.

Another thing that has helped is knowing about vicarious trauma: important for us to know about. Like Al-Anon. It's very similar to people who have lived with alcoholics. Do what I need to do to stay healthy.

When I start to feel triggered and want to blow up, I go for a walk. When I feel like pigging out, I try now to go into the other room and burn that energy off on the exercise bike. Or when I start to feel bad, I get on that phone list of other vet wives. My family and friends don't understand…they think I'm talking French to them. I want to talk with someone I know understands. Just have that connection.

Bottom line: I am setting some priorities in my life and I'm gonna do what I have to do.

❧

There are some deep things that no one knows about my vet. When I feel all alone, like no one understands these secrets, I want others in the same situation to know they're not alone in their hard times. In fact, Jack and I were out to dinner tonight and were just talking about his inner struggles. At least now he can speak about some of the harder issues, where in the past he couldn't even accept that he had a problem in some areas of his life. Maybe there is room for progress.

❧

It took me years to realize that when they blow up at us, sometimes they have no conscious knowledge of how they are treating us. I used to think he was really cruel and was doing it deliberately. But after the storm he almost didn't even know what I was talking about. Sure was baffling! We can't fix them, but we can help them be aware of when they're starting to escalate. My job is to tune in to me and my reactions and not fuel the fire. But it helps when I tell him, "I feel a little anxious right now. You're like a ticking time bomb. Are you okay? Is there anything I can do to help?" Sometimes it helps and sometimes it doesn't, but at least I'm not getting dumped on and attacked all the time now. I also am getting better at learning when to get out of the way. He always seems to come back and be okay again eventually. It helps me to remember that part.

❧

As a mother of a veteran with PTSD, I have really struggled. I feel so help-less. He's not making good choices. It's hard to know when to be a mom and when to let go. One thing that worked well was that I connected with a support group. I found lots of resources. Among them was the name and number of a veteran who helps others with PTSD. Rather than calling him and asking him to talk to my son, I gently passed on the information to my son and encouraged him to consider just giving the guy a call. Just to talk. Nothing else. And then let my son decide where to go from there. I can provide resources for him and even gently bribe him (motivate him?), but then I have to let go. And to keep my boundaries. To not let him get to me if he's not first willing to take the steps to take care of himself. And I pray for him. A lot.

❧

We both need to be aware of our anxiety as it creeps up; sometimes just talking about it helps. "I'm starting to feel anxious …"

❧

The only way they can survive is God. There are a lot of guilt issues. He thinks, "I'm bad." He doubts that what he did could ever be forgiven. Also, he cannot give more than he does. There is a hole in their lives. They can't feel. They are so limited. We both have to lean on God.

❧

Fixing says: "You're not okay until you get better."

❧

Things seem to go well for awhile then kaboom! We have to remember to watch for the triggers. I forget to keep alert for them, or at least mildly aware at all times. Each of us has to discover the unique triggers for our vets. This is something we can do—and must do. It really makes a difference in not letting things escalate. It is in my power to choose to not let things escalate. Ted and I were at each other's throats the other day and I just fed the fire. He blew and then I blew. It was awful. Then later I realized and recognized that all the triggers had been adding up during the week. So I'm seeing how much better things go when I can be the one to keep things calm.

❧

We all need each other.

❧

Sometimes I just want to walk out. But I can't. I have no place to go. We're financially locked together and I feel trapped. But maybe if I explore some options I might be able to if I really need to. I guess I just want it to be perfect and it probably never will be.

❧

We cannot let our fear of their response stop us from speaking what we need and want.

❧

As a single mother of a veteran on a limited income, I've had some struggles. In addition to the pain and anguish that it brings to see my son in so much distress, I struggle with not being able to help him more. And him not taking my advice (well that is not new). He lives with me because he can't afford anywhere else. That is hard. He depends a lot on me and I think he needs to be out on his own.

I'm glad he went through the VA program. It has helped a lot. But he has more stuff going on. So I need to find the best way to help him with life but not let him invade mine. He's a grown-up now and I will continue to help him go forward with his life in a positive way.

❦

Among other things, I'm working on *not* being the caregiver for the world. It's my nature to listen, help, be there, protect, and nurture everyone who crosses my path. I don't think that's a bad thing.

But I have to learn to depend on others besides myself at times. Finding support from others has really made a difference—even though it took everything I had to step out and seek it. Those who understand and can give wise advice and caring have been helping me tremendously. I think I've been a little bit mad at God too because things have been so terribly hard and not at all the way I had planned for my life to go. I'm very ashamed to admit this, and I'm working on rebuilding my faith and trust in Him. I'm the one who left Him. He never left me.

❦

I need to be more aware of how much I'm trying to draw my energy and life from my vet, rather than nourishing myself.

❦

I have been observing my vet and others for awhile now. I know that everyone is different, but I see something really important that my vet has that makes a difference in our relationship. And that has made it possible for us to stay together all these years. He has God in his life. He has a good heart. A tender heart. That makes it possible for him to learn and grow and apologize and then go on. Of course, I need to do those things too. But how precious to have a man who is not ashamed to humble himself and ask God for help.

❦

It seems all to be so overwhelming.

He will never be completely free of this scar.

Last Tuesday I had a meltdown in the car while riding down the street. I had awakened that day feeling crowded, claustrophobic, nervy, irritable, like crying and getting angry. Not even sure why, just stuff had collected inside me that I probably had not processed in a good way. As I had learned growing up where feelings were not allowed to be expressed, I just stoically held it in. Unfortunately on the road, it all just exploded out.

"I feel like I'm going to either explode or implode!"

My husband immediately pulled the car over into a parking lot, turned it off, reached over, and wrapped his arms around me. And then he prayed. For me. Wow. What a beautiful moment. I needed him and didn't even realize how much. Up until then, I had felt like I was maybe pushing him away...now he was my comfort. It was me all along, not him. I realized later that my hormones were all off-kilter and I lost sleep and was really on edge.

What I learned that day was to express my feelings, and not feel like I needed to know the solution. But to let him into my pain. The same way I'm close to him in his. Many of our vets have compassion deep inside of them and it is a strength waiting to be tapped into.

As a child, I was never allowed to express feelings. Never heard! Not safe! If ever I did, it was "fixed" immediately. Not allowed to just express it. Now I can. I am heard. I can say how I feel and not need to know the answer.

Also, when he comforts me, it is good for *him*! It gets him outside of himself and brings us close. So either of us can comfort the other, and we both come out winners.

❧

We can't wait until they're stable for us to be stable.

❧

Compassion is a companion to understanding.

❧

This PTSD thing is still new to me, even after a few years of knowing about it. I just had an "ah-ha" moment today! Several years ago, when our relationship was about a year old, I almost threw in the towel. He had a major, really devastating cave day (actually it was more like about a week). Now we refer to them as cave days, but at the time we didn't know more than just to dread the episodes.

That day was going great until the evening when he told me he needed some time alone. Basically, he didn't want to see me, not even call me, for awhile. I was crushed! Wanted to beat him up and also sob at the same time. I just stood there blankly. In shock. "What?" Then he said quietly that it was not me but it was him. Yea, right. Heard that before.

I went home and flew into a rage. Took the "I Love You" balloon he had given me and beat it to pieces. Then it really ticked me off because it was a musical balloon. Every time I hit it harder, it started the annoying song again. Finally, I just stomped on it and it died.

I felt like I had died, too. What was that horrible overpowering rage? And I felt such grief. Such anger, fear, loneliness, rejection.

The next few days were awful. I tried to reason it out, but this was unlike any relationship problem I had ever experienced. Where was he and why did he pull away and push me away? And he had just told me he loved me the day before!!

Fast-forward to the present. We're now married and both of us have gotten counseling and read all we could get our hands on about PTSD. We're growing and taking each day as it comes. I'm so glad we didn't give up. It has taken both of us—and God.

Going back through my journal I remembered that incident back then (strangely enough I still kept the smashed annoying balloon). Yesterday he told me that it was on that day years ago that was his first day in combat. The plane took him and dropped him off right in the middle of the war! Terror. Bombs. Dead bodies. The horrors are too much to take in.

I get it now. The cave he goes into, not by his choice, is the only way he can survive the lifelong effects of his trauma. And this is just one ("anniversary" they call it).

I do see now that this had nothing to do with me. Really. Now I have to remember that and let him go into his cave when he needs to and not take it personally. I try to do good things for me and get stuff on my "to-do" list done during this time.

Eventually he does come out. And I welcome him with open arms.

❧

"It's my turn!"

❧

They have their problems, but when it hits the fan we would want to be in a room full of vets. They would know what to do. If push comes to shove, they can be some of the strongest people. It's a good thing. These guys with PTSD are some of the strongest-hearted guys. They come across as hard and tough, but they are deep. They have real big hearts. They are kind.

Because they're so thoughtful and caring, their trauma has really messed them up. He told me about the stuff that went on. It was so horrible and I just couldn't take it. Let alone imagine that he has to live with it forever. When he first told me about the stuff that went on, I went and had a glass of wine. And I don't drink!

Grounded wives provide love from a position of strength. As we get grounded in the best of ourselves, we can be fully present to our vet in crisis.

I wonder if pain is the seed that turns hearts into gold.

My vet and I were good friends in high school. Then we got married and soon he went to Afghanistan. When he came back, he was really different. Kind of weird, but I just brushed it off and we kept going. We had our little girls soon after that. Then he started really showing problems. Drinking, tremendous anger, and rage. Then drugs. Then threatening suicide. It was the most horrible time of my life—our lives. Then we got help. We both learned about PTSD. He's doing better but still has his moments. I don't know if there is a God and I don't pray much, but I'm glad others were willing to pray for us. One thing that has made a difference is that he now volunteers and helps other veterans and active-duty military families.

This is crazy. I love him, but I can't go on with all of this anymore. I need to make some changes in me.

We had such a hard time at night. He would wake me up screaming out in the middle of the night about bloody body parts and putting pieces or arms together. I still cry when I think about what he went through.

And that is just the stuff he tells me. My heart hurts for him. I wish I could make it all go away. But I can't. I can love him and hold him.

✍

I need to see my triggers, too, and find a strategy for me.

✍

When he puts up his walls and refuses my affection it really hurts. Like heck. I want to die inside and cry and hit him. How can he refuse the very thing he desperately needs? I'm learning that I have to let go and realize he is who he is; but I am me. It is not my fault. Wallowing in self-pity or rage does not help *me*. Each time that happens, I have to go forward…for me. What really helps is to go for a walk alone…rain or shine. This has been one of the best things I can do.

✍

I do not stop living even if he does.

✍

You have to find those little windows where you can safely talk.

✍

The hardest thing for me has been his withdrawing. My heart would ache every time my vet pulled away. Sometimes it was physical, like when he actually disappeared for a few days without warning and without telling anyone where he was. Other times it was emotional. It was as if he wasn't even in his body. For years I just felt dead, terribly alone, and so confused. Finally with the help of my counselor I'm learning to be strong, to take care of me, and to build my life in a healthy way regardless of his ability to be present. I'm also realizing that the healthier I am and the more stable I am, the easier it is for him to come back.

❧

Once I started seeing things through his eyes, things began to change; not sure how, but maybe the change began in me.

❧

I married him, knowing he was wounded and handicapped. It makes it harder because the handicap is invisible. If I could see him with no arms, it might make it easier to remember his condition.

❧

I was widowed at a young age and kind of in a fog for years. I had three young children at the time. Then I met my vet who was riddled with PTSD but didn't know it at the time. Because he was a medic, he experienced trauma every day. Looking back, I see that technically every day is an anniversary for him. So it's understandable that he drank very heavily. He was a drunk. And it took its toll on all of us. Al-Anon really helped me then. I went regularly. After a DUI, which really scared him, he stopped drinking.

We are going on thirty-six years now. One thing that we learned was that he had to learn that when I cried, all he could do was hold me. That really helped. Both of us can hold each other, but we cannot fix the hurts. Sometimes holding is just what we need.

Becoming a Christian later in life helped a lot. He has changed over the years but still has episodes.

Everyone thought I was this incredibly strong dynamic woman, but down deep inside I wasn't. Nobody could see that. I felt scared. I had to put on the front. Fear was the biggest motivator.

My awareness of what I needed began when I went to college at an older age and started to accomplish things in my own life. This was something I did that was significant in my own mind. As my self-esteem grew, it helped him understand that I am a person too. I'm not a target for his stress. Many of us set ourselves up to be targets.

I realized that I want him even though I no longer technically needed him. That was a freeing and empowering thought to me. I could now choose.

I've spent a lot of time with other women and family members in similar situations. If I had to narrow it down after all these years, the only thing that works is to take care of ourselves. We are caregivers, enablers and often totally lacking in self-confidence. Many vet wives believe they don't deserve to be treated any differently. For some who were abused earlier in their lives, when the PTSD enters their lives it is a familiar place. We can slip right into it again. Taking care of us is paramount.

The other thing is boundaries. They are so important. This helps our self-esteem and helps us take care of us. It's okay. We can do it in a healthy way. We will still have baggage, but at least we have tools to help us cope.

The only way to make a go of it is to become self-aware and improve your self-image so that you feel better about yourself. Really understand that the key is you. Like they say at Al-Anon, this is my illness coinciding with his. As soon as I was able to see this perspective, I started getting well.

⚘

I think I'm in this marriage and have been stuck for so long because I don't have enough respect for myself to get out, or to stand up for myself to him. I always seem to beat myself up when he gets mad at me, thinking it was something I did. Maybe if I get some help and grow stronger, I can be healthier and safer. And then maybe he'll start to treat me better. I have to do something soon. I think it's time now. I deserve it.

❦

I was so looking forward to having everybody over for Christmas. All the kids and grandkids. A houseful for three days. Yippee! I love it! But he could not take it. Too much stress. The good news is that over the years I've learned how to make both of us happy. He can take it (people and noise and commotion in his house) for a little while; then I plan outings for everyone. Movies, malls, etc. And then he can have some peace and quiet at home alone. Everyone stays in better moods that way. I think sometimes we need to be a little more creative in finding ways that meet both of our needs.

❦

Why do I feel so terribly alone? Loneliness is one of the most painful emotions. I want to love and be loved. And that is why I got together with him. Little did I realize that the PTSD would drive a wedge between us. Sometimes the loneliness is bad because he has cut me off in anger. The worst is when he withdraws from me. He either takes off for a few days or just goes into a depression. He doesn't even respond to me. It's like either he is dead or I am. I can't take that. I just want to run away. Or even think about ending things. It really hurts.

The only thing that helps me is to pray and also try to find someone else who understands. I wish I had more people who understood.

❦

I feel so good. After all these years of putting up walls (both of us) and yelling (both of us), I have decided I'm not going to live that way anymore. It has been taking away my self-worth. I hate to withdraw. I sort of shrivel up and wither. So I'm discovering that as scary as it is, I do better when I can keep calm and suggest we talk about things. We are actually communicating now and I like it! And the more I do it, the easier it is. Still scary, but getting better. This could really be a good thing!

I don't know what I'd do without our wives and family support group. I come with a heavy load and it always gets lifted. Some of the ladies are a little strange, but maybe they think I am too. We understand each other. We speak the same language. And there's a common bond. I always go away with something encouraging. And always see someone who has it a lot worse than I do. In between the meetings it is comforting to know I'll be seeing them soon, and the urgency and loneliness is easier to take.

Hey…we're all going to get through this!

I need to own my own stuff. But so does he. Sometimes it seems like he just doesn't even know he's acting in a certain way. How can he grow if he can't even acknowledge what he is doing? So I'm learning to speak up when I feel that chill go down my spine. That's the worst and scariest time to speak up, but I am doing it. And surviving! Kind of feels good. Sure don't like that freak-out feeling, but I'm doing it anyway. And sometimes it helps him realize what's going on before it gets out of hand. Each time I do it, it seems to get a little easier.

Never underestimate the immeasurable value of your love and ministry to your veteran! You are irreplaceable. God put each of us here for a reason, if *only* to love and care for this one person, the person of God's choosing.

❦

When I find myself going into a downward negative spiral, I can turn it around by making him a card, listing a whole bunch of things I love about him. Aim high. You'll be pleasantly surprised at the change in you, not to mention the response in his heart.

❦

I want to say something to all of the others in my support group: It means so much to me that you accept me as I am. Thank you.

❦

I can choose to love. I can choose to take care of me. Both are blessings. How he responds is up to him. But either way, I am better off when I love.

❦

What is this feeling that I'm not allowed to feel happy when he I not… sort of that I feel compelled to match his moods? Why does it seem that when he gets set off, it only takes seconds before I "match" him? Sometimes I wonder if I have PTSD, too.

I hate struggling so hard with these emotions day after day. I wish I could be more stable and unique in myself so that his ups and downs don't make me go up and down with him.

I hate feeling so reflective of him. It seems like I'm only a mirror. I want to be strong and compassionate and loving and healthy but feel dragged down when he is. We're out of sync and we both sense it.

I need the help of someone higher than myself, whether God or other people who understand. My prayer is that I can take care of me and communicate what I need, as well as remember to have compassion for him. I need to remember that he's struggling with his PTSD and most of this is not about me. I need to live my life and reclaim the joy and energy that I had a few days ago.

✿

Our vets have brains that need healing. Our loving touches throughout the day and night can get through to them more than any drug ever could. They also have huge hearts, just like we do. And we all need to be loved. Never underestimate the power and blessing of a simple loving touch.

✿

We are walking miracles.

✿

I would love to support him any way I can and hear the perspectives of others whose loved ones also suffer from PTSD. I want to learn. I'll do anything for this relationship. He means the world to me.

✿

It touched me so much when my husband said to me, "Nothing else matters except that we have the Lord and we have each other." I cannot think of anything he has ever said that has reached so deeply into my soul. I hope he remembers he said that.

✿

I need to get grounded.

✿

My husband has been really down since yesterday. Things have been so good for so long that I am surprised. I guess I shouldn't be. I haven't seen him like that in a long time. I had forgotten the pull, the drag it has on me. I pray for God to help him. And help me to live my joyous life, and not get sucked down with fear or self-doubts or the compulsion to fix him.

✍❤

My vet and I are in our second year together. We are just discovering all about PTSD. I'm so glad he's willing to get help. Me too! I'm really excited and I hope he finds some peace and direction.

✍❤

One of the things that helps me is to write. I have journaled off and on but not much recently. It's a very good thing during these days of grieving for Dad, as well as caring for Mom and a husband with PTSD.

✍❤

We are the strong ones.

✍❤

I just don't get it. Why does he spend so much time playing violent video games? He's almost addicted to them. I don't understand why those who have lived through the horror of violence want to spend all their time being entertained by it. But I do not nag. The best thing for me is to try to talk with him about it and get him to open up and tell me more. But sometimes he just shuts me out and dives into this fantasy world. I wonder if it's because now he is in control. He can conquer the enemy. So I try not to be bothered by it, but I do ask him to spend some time with me and the kids so he's not always obsessed with the gaming.

My first task is to regulate me (calm myself down). Regulating me is coming back to the place where I can breathe and think and feel. Coming back to a center, as they say. Or for me it's kind of like being a tree with solid roots. Then I can think and am more in control of what I say and do. The good part is that I don't have to apologize as much!

For a long time I've struggled with how to keep the communication open yet not allow him to dump his negativity on me. I feel angry, resentful, and depressed when he is negative. Part of that is my own tendency to feel responsible to keep him happy. I want to be caring but not enslaved to his moods. One night I really felt the resentment building. I'm getting better at recognizing it. Honestly, I didn't want to be with him; yet I felt afraid to say anything for fear that he would pull back. So I mustered up the courage and decided to speak. I don't want to feel like a helpless child.

So I gently but clearly asked him, "I love it when you share with me and I want to keep the communication open, but sometimes I feel like you're really negative and it gets to me. I feel overwhelmed. What would you like me to do when I feel I'm being dumped on?"

I was prepared for the worst. But his response was pleasantly surprising. He responded very kindly, "Have I been doing that?"

Bracing a little bit, I replied, "Yes. The last two days have been a lot of whining about the rain, the mud, gays, the TV, etc."

He paused. Did not get triggered (hooray!) and then answered, "Then just do what you just did and tell me."

That simple? Well it was a start anyway in the right direction. I know the more I can speak honestly and openly, the better we will both be. It felt good to speak and not hold it in, and especially not to explode. I need wisdom and grace.

I've noticed in the groups I've participated in that the ladies who have a faith in God are more successful in staying with their vet and using God as their resource for strength. The ladies who weren't connected to God were the ones who were the most angry or desperate, and had no hope, outside of hoping that the VA could help their men. Most weren't even considering their own reactions and behaviors. At least I know that for me I would be long gone without that faith and life.

It's really good for our vets to help others. As my vet does that, I see the result of helping others is helping him too. And although he'll always have it, he is no longer trapped by the PTSD. I encourage him to volunteer as much as he can.

I know we can't fix them. But one thing that has helped us both is when I help him help himself. The other day he was moping around, feeling pretty down. We had a nice hug, and I told him I love him. But I still wanted to fix him. Then and there. Darn!

Realizing that was not possible, nor necessary, I thought of something: How about if I asked him what he needs? Rather than just sitting by while he spiraled downward, and rather than telling him all the things I thought he should do, I posed a question. "What do you need today?"

He had no idea. So I let him ponder that for awhile; then I made a couple of suggestions, one of which was how about some nice music on his favorite CD. He jumped up and ran into the family room, put the CD on, and sat down. A few minutes later he was bumbling around the house humming and doing stuff. His mood was on the way up.

And all I had to do was love him and encourage him to think about his needs and all the good things he could do for himself.

The more we can tune in to what our body is trying to tell us, the better we'll be able to grow stronger in the chaos.

It's not about figuring it all out and getting the answers and having it done with. It's a lifelong process. Learning and growing together.

We can't expect our husbands to meet all our needs (no husband can!). Sometimes we think he is God and he can read our minds—that he can supply all the emotional comfort and support we crave. He is just him. Love him for who he is.

We long for our man to be our protector…but in many ways he cannot. He's just barely getting through each day as it is. He wants to take care of us, but his resources are so limited. Ironically, we find ourselves taking care of him. We have become the strong one. Some of us have lost touch with our tender feminine side and can resent not having him be there for us.

But that is an ideal world. And we're learning to make the most of what we do have. To take care of us and to enjoy him as much as possible.

One thing that helps a lot is to focus on where I can get my needs met. Such as do I have a close friend or two? We can't forget to cherish and cultivate our female friendships! We can giggle and cry and play and talk deeply. We can eat out and do goofy girl things together.

And then we are recharged and can go back home and love him to pieces!

Faith, hope, and love are the key.

❧

We got off to a bad start. We were married young and he had PTSD. And we both drank. Not a good combination. Things went downhill. And stayed downhill. Not sure why I didn't get out, but I guess I never thought I had options.

Until one day I realized I did. And maybe my life depended on it. I was terrified. How could I just leave? I had my own issues to deal with first. So I got help and I got sober. It wasn't easy. I went to counseling and I went to AA. But it was good. He didn't like that. And he kept on in his bad ways and lots of PTSD stuff, too.

Things got worse. I got more frustrated. Well, scared spitless actually. So after many weeks of gearing up for it and planning, I told him if he didn't stop drinking and start treating me better, I would leave. He didn't believe me. Two days later, when he was at work, I gathered all my stuff with the help of my friends and left. I cried so hard. I felt so bad. So alone. So grief-ridden. I kept wondering if I had done something wrong.

I stayed temporarily at my friend's house while I gathered my thoughts and tried to figure out my next step. I was so tempted to go back to where it was familiar, even though it was unhealthy and danger-ous at times.

Well, surprise of surprises. He only lasted two days. He came crawl-ing to me, begging for me to come home. He couldn't take it without me. I was stunned and so relieved and so excited…and so not trusting. So I told him that if he started going to AA and got help at the VA with counseling and a support group, I would come home as soon as I saw he was actually doing those things.

Wow. I still look back and see how amazing that was. But I had to take care of myself first. I had to do the hard thing. I had to do the scary thing. And be willing to take whatever consequences happened.

Believe it or not, we have now been married for thirty-six years and both have been sober for seventeen. He still has PTSD and always will. But we love each other and we deal with it. Without the alcohol, life is definitely more than just doable. It is good.

✍

I know this sounds weird, but the more attentive I am to my internal signals, the less likely I am to go out of my body and become part of him when he's not doing well. Does that make sense?

✍

Remember your individuality.

✍

I find myself constantly tuned to what he will need next and to provide it for him when he does. I get to the point where I almost forget me when I'm consumed by thinking about him. As if I could preempt trouble by staying ahead of the game. It gets so tiring.

Rather, I should help him learn to get in touch with his own needs. I can be a reflector. Ask him, "Honey, what do you need right now?" I've cultivated his dependency on me. I can turn that around and help him take responsibility. He's capable of learning to tune in to his needs. I can remind him and make suggestions. But don't do it for him.

And for me on the flip side, I need to be more aware of my own needs and wants. And feel free to meet them. I can and must ask for what I need.

✍

The tears come off and on throughout life, but I'm so glad this world is not my home, and I know one day there will be no more tears. What a hope. Thanks for the warm hugs.

✍

When I first started dating Jake, he was up-front with me about his

PTSD. That was the beginning of my journey into the land of intense ups and downs. It scared me, but for some reason I continued to fall more deeply in love with him. I began to learn more about PTSD and about the war itself. It was very helpful to take a class at the VA and to read what they had to offer. But I still doubted if I could make a lifelong commitment to this man and his disability.

The hardest part for me was when he would go into his cave and totally disconnect from me for days. It took me a long time to realize that I was not the problem. Thankfully, I had been going to counseling before I met him. My counselor (funny coincidence) was already experienced and involved with PTSD vets. His heart was as wise as his mind. And he provided much good coaching for me the entire time. I learned the importance of connecting with the one you love. I also revived my spiritual connection of faith in God and my relationship with Him. Looking back, I never could have made it without Him.

A year and half went by and I was almost ready to commit. I had seen him at his worst and best. He had a heart of gold and was truly in love with me. He also had shown true character and genuine faith in God. Still we were both terrified. Neither of us had had successful marriages before and we were determined never again to feel the devastation of divorce.

One night he surprised me by proposing to me. He lovingly handed me a dictionary where he had cut out the words "divorce" and "abandonment." I was in shock and could not answer. All night long I was torn in agony. I prayed and prayed. I deeply wanted to say yes, but I was so afraid that I couldn't measure up to the demands of a PTSD vet wife.

After a seemingly endless night, I got up early. I went outside to get some fresh morning air. Looking up I was especially drawn to one beautiful tall evergreen tree. It seemed to calm me. I prayed some more. "God, please, please show me what to do." As I continued to gaze up at that strong peaceful tree, it came to me: "Go love Jake with My love. There will always be enough."

Wow. I was overwhelmed and relieved. That was the answer I really wanted. But insecure as I am, I questioned, "Really?" And then I got the same answer. "Go love Jake with My love. There will always be enough."

I could tell you countless stories of how God's love truly has always been enough. At times it didn't seem like it, but when my love runs out, His fills me up. I cannot do this alone. But with God it has been amazing. Beautiful. Growing. Exciting. Definitely not dull. I'm so glad I am married to Jake. And he is too.

⁊

I often get to the place where I say, "I just can't do this anymore." Then I do something good for myself in a good way and pray a lot. And somehow I can do it.

⁊

The power is in the love.

⁊

When I refer to his PTSD as "the PTSD," it helps us see it as something we both share rather than a big ugly growth on his face. It seems to free him up more to be able to deal with it. Together we can do this. We have hope.

⁊

It's hardest to love someone when that love is not returned. But I hope in time it all will be worth it. At least I know it's the right thing to do. And I feel better when I am loving.

⁊

When you're angry, your brain shuts off. I do better when I'm aware of my anger and deal with it immediately so my brain doesn't shut off.

❦

Shame on me for not having more fun! If I look for it, I will find joy in my day. And if it doesn't come knocking at my door, then I can make it fun! If I mope around, then it's my own fault. But when I find people to laugh with and love and enjoy the day with, then everything is so much better!

❦

When I met my husband-to-be, I was immediately attracted by his smile, personality, and optimism. He was outgoing, friendly, and fun—everything I had ever wanted in a companion. Our relationship quickly developed and we fell in love. What I was not aware of was his deep-seated psychological issues that would affect our lives on an ongoing, almost daily basis.

Explosive, uncontrollable outbursts; recurring (nightly) nightmares; abnormal reactions to loud noises (fireworks, gunshots, car backfires, or dropped dishes); inability to have "normal" social relationships with friends; difficulty in holding a job; detachment from family; inability to believe that he is a good person; becoming enraged from incidental occurrences. These are just some examples of what we live with.

In addition to serving as a Marine in Desert Storm, he is also a Vietnam War orphan. His father was killed in action and his mother was not able to deal with the loss of a husband and birth of child. Abandonment was present in his life from day one.

Barely out of high school, he enlisted in the USMC, which I believe was the catalyst for the place where he finds himself today. Training to kill, to never show emotion, and to survive at all costs cannot be undone.

Eighteen years later, after much prodding and insistence by me, my husband finally agreed to attend a PTSD group and talk with an individual counselor. We also meet together with a marriage counselor, which is really helping me understand what he's going through and helping him understand the effect his anger, isolationism, and rage have upon me and our children.

Knowing nothing about PTSD until the past couple of months, I'm embarrassed to say that I was skeptical of the disorder. I come from a family where you "just get over things." If I could change one thing, I would be more understanding and supportive of his problems.

PTSD takes a toll on everyone. My husband has lost jobs because of his temper and inability to see any way other than his, resulting in financial distress for our family. We've had countless arguments/fights/altercations due to his explosive temper. Much of the time we're all walking on eggshells around him because we never know what will set him off.

However, the thing that is most difficult for me is to watch the self-loathing that occurs after one of his outbursts. He's always remorseful and apologetic; many times he'll break down and cry. It is the saddest thing in the world to watch a grown man, someone you love more than anything, to be in this condition.

I believe that with time, counseling, and most of all, help from God, we'll be able to manage this. I know it's something we'll have to live with always, and that is okay. The one thing that has become crystal clear throughout this whole process is that God is with us, always. And, as we believe in our house, "I can do all things through Christ who strengthens me."

These men and women are among the greatest there are. They selflessly served in wars and conflicts—popular and unpopular—to ensure freedom, democracy, and the quality of life that we all enjoy. We owe them love, support, and whatever else we must endure to let them know their sacrifice was not in vain.

&

When my stomach is in knots, then I know something is wrong.

&

You may always have to walk on eggshells to some degree. Don't let it stop you from living and being you.

✐

We all tell each other that love and compassion win the day. Unfortunately we are not always loving. We are human and have our own deep needs too. We also screw up and sometimes hurt each other. So where does that love come from? Where do I find it when it's all gone, and I need some myself? What I see from those around me who are making it work (and what works for me when I remember) is that we need a source. We need a spiritual source, a center from which the good stuff can flow. The love cannot come from nowhere. It needs to come from a spiritual source. And then I get some too!

✐

When I met my vet, he had already been through two divorces. Both of his wives rejected him. He was devastated and leery of trying it again. He had only recently learned about PTSD. He was getting help and participating in a support group. I wonder if they had known about it and been able to work with it, if both of those prior marriages would have succeeded.

So now it's my turn. I am thrilled to be the one to love him. I'm so motivated to have a happy marriage. And so is he. It really helps to have God in the picture and to have so much more understanding of the PTSD. At least we know what the elephant in the room is. Each day we both grow and don't take each other for granted. I cherish my wounded warrior and want to make up for a lifetime of love to him.

✐

Well, I learned something yesterday. And it was more than just about potatoes. PTSD does not have options. But when they relax, they can see.

I had just returned from a trip and was tired and hungry. And exhausted. Maybe hormonal too. In my great wisdom, I had asked my husband the day before to get some vegetable soup out of the freezer so I could have it when I got home. Smart, eh?

So I went into the kitchen. As it was, I was close to a meltdown just from being so tired and hungry. Eagerly I plopped the soup into a pan to heat. But alas…I saw it had potatoes in it! I had frozen two batches of soup, one with potatoes for him and one for me since I can't eat potatoes. That was the last straw needed to ignite my meltdown. Frantically I clawed my way through the freezer in search of another container of soup that did not have potatoes. Packages of frozen food were flying all over and landing with thuds on the floor. I didn't care. I was panicked. I needed food!

Hearing the commotion, my husband hurried in, wrapped his arms around me, and I sobbed. "I'm so hungry. And I'm so tired. So hungry and so tired." I could not think. I was so triggered all I could do was sob. I was sure I would die of starvation right there in the kitchen.

Well, I did calm down eventually. And I found something else to eat (I survived). And what a precious husband I have to comfort me in my distress! Looking back, I see he didn't try to "fix" me, just love me. Just like I try to do with him when he is activated. Be there to comfort and help them relax.

You know what I realized the next day—after I had lots of sleep? I could have picked out the potatoes that were in that soup and eaten it without the potatoes! Wow. How obvious, you say? Well, to someone who is not triggered and in the throes of a PTSD episode, yes. Otherwise, no. PTSD cannot see the options. We have to calm down first and then the brain can work.

I learned a little more compassion that day. A little more appreciation for my husband. And a little more motivation to broaden my culinary escapades.

✍

Don't say anything in a fit of emotion…our vets will shut off.

✐❧

All I have to do is get through today. I am going to be okay!

✐❧

I'm not responsible for anyone else's happiness—not my boss, my mother, or even my husband. On the flip side, no one else is responsible for my happiness. I have the power to stop and smell the flowers. I have the choice to sing a song anytime! I can hug someone anytime! I can go up to my vet at any moment of the day and tell him I love him. If I miss the blessings of today because I'm too focused on tomorrow, or distracted by the clock, or am in performance mode of some kind, it's my own fault.

✐❧

I can wait to speak until I am together and until he is doing well. I don't have to spill my guts on impulse. Later is often better.

✐❧

The day after a horrible conflict between us, he came up to me in the kitchen. He was very concerned and asked me if I thought he had a personality disorder. He seemed afraid. Rather than just blurt out an answer, I asked him if he thought he did and why he'd asked. He said, "All the weirdness yesterday and all the stuff that went on."

Remembering love is action and remembering compassion, and remembering not to let my baggage trigger me, I hugged him and said, "I think it's the PTSD. We forget you have it because you have so many good days. I think it affects you when you get stressed, and things trigger you. We forget that you have PTSD."

Then he asked, "Do you still love me?" Wow. Wow. He's afraid he will lose me!

"Yes, of course!" I assured him. But I also told him it is important that we are able to talk about things. He kissed me and smiled. We both felt free.

I learned later that anxiety can make a person think he's going crazy. We can help them know they're not crazy. I think that is one of their big fears.

Looking back at the situation, I see that for me my pain and anger came from the disconnect. He didn't "see me." I felt lost and alone and abandoned (all my baggage). That triggered me. His trigger came from fear that I had disconnected from him or that he would lose control and then lose me. Bottom line, we all need each other. Sometimes our actions look like we're pushing each other away, but down deep inside we all crave that love and closeness.

✍❧

When I take care of myself, he begins to get better.

✍❧

The only reason we've been married thirty-eight years is because we both have grown. I would not have stayed if he had not gotten better. Abuse and alcohol is not okay.

✍❧

Don't assume the problem is all theirs and they have to change; but communicate, "*We* have a problem; let's look at this together." This approach opens up the possibilities and keeps defenses down.

✍❧

I don't want to be fat! I just learned that the cortisol that comes from too much stress causes weight gain. So now I am really motivated, if for no other reason than to calm down. To do what I can to stay mellow. Learning to relax more and not get all worked up will help me not get so fat! I like that diet.

✍♥

It feels selfish of me to think of myself after all he's been through, but you're right. I can do nothing for anyone if I'm laid out.

✍♥

Last week I was feeling good. Frisky. I went into the family room to flirt with him, to connect after a busy day. I went in wearing only the red spaghetti apron. He just kept watching TV. I said "Hi." He looked up and then kept watching. (Aside from a few sags and wrinkles and dimples, for an old broad I don't have too bad of a body.) I told him I'd do a special spaghetti dance for him, to which he replied, "This is a really interesting program about this airplane." He ignored me. He didn't see me.

I panicked inside, felt sick to my stomach, and then left the room. What a horrible feeling inside. I wondered if we had come to the point where it was hum drum, and the TV would win out over me. I was pretty upset inside but I held it in (not good).

The next day on my walk I realized I needed to tell him that I need his attention and affection or at least his acknowledgement of me. If it's something he wants to watch, great…just acknowledge me, maybe with a hug and a smile, or a "Honey, I love you. Here, wanna come join me we can watch this together." Just see me. Connect! I feel like falling apart when he doesn't. I feel like nobody.

A few days later I told him that his affection and attention are very important to me—that I never want to have to compete with the TV. Immediately with a smile he answered, "Oh, that would never happen. You're number one."

Well, I don't know from day to day when he'll be "there" or not. But I can keep reaching out and being me. One more thought: I thought about it in reverse. When he walks into the room, do I stop what I'm doing and acknowledge him? Do I respond with joy? Wow. I want to be sure to do that!

✧

Fear makes us lose our closeness with our loved one. We are no longer connected when we are afraid of someone. There is no sharing of emotion. But when I choose to love, the connection happens. Loving and caring brings healing.

✧

Sometimes I feel like my son died over there, and this person who came back is a shadow, a cheap imitation of who he was. I miss him so much. What would I do without the privilege of praying for him? That seems like it's all I can do. Maybe it's more than I realize. Maybe it's the best thing I can do.

✧

A few years ago I made a commitment in my mind but didn't tell anyone. Every time my husband came home from somewhere, I planned to meet him at the door and welcome him as if he had just come home from the war. Wow! What a difference that has made! I get excited now when I hear him coming, and we both treasure our at-the-door kisses and hugs. He is now getting the welcome he has deserved all his life.

✧

I could very much use someone to connect with who understands this awful PTSD thing. I'm desperate for the connection. All the stress and chaos has caused me to become so forgetful and unfocused. I am unable to afford "real" counseling and really prefer to talk to others.

❧

It seems like emotional change is the name of every day.

❧

My biggest struggle is that my husband is severely disabled physically. He continues to go downhill, as both of his feet have been amputated and his organs and cognitive functions are fading. I don't feel like a wife anymore. I miss him. Being his caretaker has caused me to distance myself just so I can perform the necessary daily tasks. I love him dearly and he loves me. But things are so different now. The only way I can survive is with God's help. Lots of prayer and promises from His words. Also, my other lifelines are my support groups, the Love Our Vets group, as well as the caregivers' support. I have to remember to look for the joyful moments, and when I can to make the joyful moments. The most precious thought that keeps me going is that he would do all of this for me in a heartbeat.

❧

I know how easily he can slip back into the Never Never Land of PTSD. He can become so remote, unwilling to give, unwilling to talk, start up the substance abuse. I guess that's kind of the name of the game for vet wives though. And I will hang in there.

❧

I was frantic. Groping in the dark. Feeling so alone and on the verge of going crazy! Berserk. I felt I couldn't do this anymore. My son has severe, uncontrollable PTSD and his wife has a substance abuse problem, therefore I have the little grandchildren. My head is truly grateful to be able to care for them, but my heart grieves that in order to do so I've had to sever relations with my son. A restraining order. It has been awful. My friends and "advisers" made me question whether I had done the right thing. I have been in turmoil. I cannot fix him! My boy. And I cannot fix these precious little children, but I can love them.

None of the people around me had a clue about PTSD, and I'm just learning. I came across the www.loveourvets.org website and contacted someone in your group. Do you know how my life was lifted that day!

They wrote back that I should take care of me, and maybe I have to let go of my son for now, but he may come around later. The children need me now. It's not an easy choice. My first concern is to be safe and to keep them safe. The adults are struggling with their stuff, but they are adults and they are choosing. Take one second, one minute, one day at a time. Then she said there is hope and many of us out here are living it!

I felt like I had reached my hand out in the terrible darkness and someone took it and held it warmly.

Thank you.

❧

Don't argue with them when they're triggered.

❧

Always be available to listen.

❧

We were married for thirty-two years before we even knew about PTSD. I always wondered what was so terribly wrong, but couldn't put my finger on it. He thought he was going crazy. So did I. Finally, he was diagnosed with PTSD. Things got a little better, but not much.

A few years later he was put on a bunch of meds by his healthcare people (no names). He got worse and worse. He was then diagnosed with Alzheimer's in addition to other things. More meds. More awful stuff. But we hung in there. I do love him.

Then one night he attacked me and did things to me that are too horrible to talk about. It was like he was not even himself. After asking God for help, I took him up to the VA hospital. There they discovered that twelve of the fifteen medications he had been on were all contraindicated for PTSD. They had totally screwed him up, and no one caught it until that night. They took him off twelve of them and guess what? I have my man back. His brain was literally shutting down because of the PTSD and improper medication, and no one realized it until then.

He still has PTSD, but he is here. He is coherent and absolutely aghast at his behavior that night. He also has started counseling and group therapy at the VA and I have joined a wives' support group. I'm so thankful that we have a second chance. Each day gets better and better.

✍❤

I'm learning when to just get out of the way—to go to my safe place.

✍❤

I feel like I have to be a referee.

✍❤

Ever notice that the things that seem like such a big deal at night are not such a big deal in the morning? That helps me not get so out of whack over each little incident. Just waiting it out often is all I need to do.

✍❤

At night I try to think of five things for which I am thankful. It helps me relax and get a better perspective. And I sleep better and I wake up better.

✍

PTSD sees no options.

✍

I met my husband while attending college. I was wanting to grow spiritually and was seeking direction for my life. My future husband had just returned from Vietnam and had been honorably discharged from the Air Force. Ted was also looking for direction and growth. We married soon after he graduated from college and then he spent twenty-eight years with United Parcel Service. He didn't exhibit signs of Posttraumatic Stress for many years, until after his retirement. He had been able to keep it buried by working hard and stuffing his emotions.

After retirement, as life slowed a little, he began to experience night terrors that gradually increased in number and intensity. As this continued, he would occasionally attack me, putting me in a choke hold, kicking, hitting, and yelling. Due to concerns for my physical safety, we chose to begin sleeping in separate bedrooms.

Meanwhile, our daughter had been praying that he would somehow find the help he needed. God answered her prayer in a very unique way. One morning Ted's behavior was very unusual and erratic. He seemed to be in a different world. When I commented on my concerns, he became combative.

He had planned to take a dresser to our daughter in his pickup. When I suggested he wait, he told me to leave him alone or he would splatter me all over the walls. I was beginning to be afraid, so I left home for awhile, which, as it turned out, was a big mistake.

When I returned home, he wasn't there. Gasoline had been spilled in the garage apparently as he removed the dresser and put it in the pickup.

At that time I didn't know where he was. I went looking for him in places he might be, including our daughter's home. Unable to locate him, I eventually called 911 and gave a description of him, indicating that he might be in need of medical attention.

Within an hour, I received a call from the police informing me that he had been involved in an auto accident and subsequently was taken to hospital emergency. He had rear-ended a car, resulting in a chain reaction involving six other cars. I called our daughter to let her know and hurried to the hospital. He was in emergency being evaluated and I was kept informed.

They wanted to know if he had a military background as he was combative at times and unresponsive at others. Eventually he was moved to ICU where he threatened to take out the whole hospital if "they don't release me." Security was called and it required three security guards to restrain him. He was difficult to sedate and eventually put on a respirator, a requirement needed for the heavy sedation necessary to calm him. He was in ICU for three days during which time he didn't indicate that he knew who his family was.

Finally, on the third day, when our daughter and I came to visit, he called us by name. What a relief it was to know that Dad and Husband—as we know him—was back. During his stay, many tests were performed, none of which explained the episode. The final diagnosis, after all other conditions were ruled out, was dissociative disorder as a result of PTSD. He began treatment with medication and counseling, all of which have really helped.

At times, PTSD is very difficult to live with and takes its toll on both of us. On occasion I've wanted to move into an apartment temporarily, just to get rest and a break from "life." Vacationing together is not restful as we must share a hotel room and bed. Ted can't have campouts with his grandchildren since his sleep difficulties are, at times, scary for them. We've explained the situation to them, but it feels like a loss not to be able to bond with them while "camping out," whether at home or in the woods.

This experience has taught me many things. First, it is imperative that I take care of myself so that I have emotional and physical reserves to help him. There are several things that soothe me, including talking to family and friends, and I try to choose the very best listeners. I've also found that I need time alone and the space to regroup on a regular basis.

This can include spiritual reflection, such as worship, meditation, and scripture reading. It can be lunch with friends, a candlelit bath with a good book, and, most especially, exercise on a regular basis. Ted and I have found that humor is good. For example, he refers to his episode as his "Parallel universe."

I treasure Ted for his gentleness and his willingness to get help. I'm proud of him for his service to country, which has taken its toll, resulting in lifelong physical and mental issues. He's a good man.

✒

You have to find those little windows where you can safely talk.

✒

Truly I can't fix this.

✒

Always remember their anniversaries. Every day of every year ask yourself if this is one.

✒

It is our choice and in our power to refrain from blurting out all our emotions. We need to take time out to process them to a point where our words and tones can be heard by them.

✒

We need to have the courage to stick up for ourselves if we're being treated badly, no matter what problems the other person may be having.

❧

I want to always learn and grow and be the person God wants me to be. If I'm stuck, it's no one's fault but my own. No one can dictate my feelings and choices. Every day I can choose to live, to learn, and to be all I can be. I do not like being angry, or critical, or controlling. I want to be loving. I am a loving person! I want to get back my sense of humor! I am a fun person! I choose each day what to be upset about…and what to be grateful for. I do not want to be critical; I want to be compassionate. I do not want to be down…or whiney…I want to be grateful.

Change can look hopeless when I look too far ahead, or when I look to another person to change. But I can choose today to take one hour just to be good to me. I can choose any time to take one hour a week to give to someone in need, visit a lonely person in a nursing home, or volunteer at a homeless shelter, etc. Then I come away grateful! Not self-absorbed—and my life has purpose.

I don't wait for anyone else to live my life; I choose not to match the mood of the person I live with. I am free to choose every day to be loving, kind, fun, etc. And I can do all this when I stay connected to my life-giver: God.

❧

When I ask Him for help He really does help.

❧

I used to be afraid, intimidated by my vet. Not anymore. Thankfully. I needed to realize that most of them are just scared. The way they act sometimes is a protection for them. Inside they are afraid. I have more compassion now than anger.

My brother was in Desert Storm. When he came back things were very different. Although I was out of the house myself, I saw how messed up he was. Because of finances he continued to live with my mom. And unfortunately he was abusive to her. He had so much anger! And he drank. None of us could understand why he had changed so much. Where was my real brother?

Eventually he moved out and in with his girlfriend. Their relationship was not very healthy. I distanced myself from him because I was afraid. I didn't know how to act around him, so I just pretended he didn't exist. But then when holidays came around, I was forced to join in the festivities.

Over time Mom became more and more distraught and my brother became more and more confused and volatile. Finally after years of this craziness, one of his friends talked him into going to the VA. Reluctantly he did. And they recommended he go into an inpatient treatment center. Six months later he returned home. I don't know exactly what went on, but I do know that he is much better. He has stopped drinking, is choosing better friends (still likes motorcycles), and he now comes to church with us.

My mother and I and have done some reading on PTSD. Now we see so much more clearly why he has such a struggle with life. I had no compassion before because I just didn't get it. I've opened up again to him and am so glad to say that we are true siblings again. I missed him. But I am here for him now. For the long haul. And Mom couldn't be happier.

Take care of *you*. Be sure to have your own space and your own "thing."

❧

We had a bad week. He had been upset by something that had happened at one of his groups related to the war. It was a hard week. But I tried to keep focused on doing good things for me and just letting him work through his stuff. I know now that it's not my fault and that I cannot change it.

At the end of the week, we were in the bathroom together and I reached out and hugged him. We just held each other. He turned to me and said, "I am very much in love with you. About my weirdness, don't hold it against me." We hugged more and I said okay.

I felt like crying and almost just swept my feelings under the rug. But instead, out it came: "I feel like crying." I didn't figure it out—just felt it and said it.

He held me tighter and said, "Go ahead and have a good cry. I felt like crying earlier today." He went on to say that he knew the last few days he had been in a bad mood because of the thing that guy said last week. We talked about it more.

So we just felt, but didn't fix. It was life-giving. And it made me feel freer and at the same time closer to him.

The more I am in this, the more I'm convinced that God designed us to connect with each other as husband and wife physically and emotionally. It's crucial and powerful!

❧

I want to continue to learn about my husband. The more I know him, the more I know how to love him. I love being a loving person. Compassion is beautiful...it sometimes hurts, but it is good. When he shared with me about not being given bullets or a functioning gun in the midst of the battle, I was so filled with compassion. It helps me understand why he does what he does today. The more I know him, the more I know how to love him.

Hope does not have to be gone. No one needs to be stuck.

What a free feeling to remember that he doesn't have to be happy all the time. How freeing! I cannot keep him happy—and I do not have to. My job is to be me and love him. His happiness is not up to me.

I am a parent of a veteran with PTSD. I believe that things happen for a reason. Many years ago I was involved in a serious accident at work that landed me in the hospital for two weeks and out of work for six months. I recall the nurse looking at me in my condition, surprised that I survived. I remember her saying, "God must have had a purpose for you to be alive." Upon returning to work I was classified as fifty percent disabled.

That planted a seed in me that changed my thinking as to what was my purpose. I looked forward and did not dwell on my disabilities. Don't be afraid to share stories with your vet that changed your life, knowing that all things happen for a reason.

It's not for us to know the reason, but to discover where this journey will take me, and how I can help someone else in a similar situation.

Much of what we experience in our marriages is normal stuff, except it becomes turbocharged when PTSD is a factor.

Sometimes things are going so well I forget he has PTSD, or I assume things have gotten better. Then it hits again.

They say that PTSD can't see options. I find myself experiencing that at times along with my vet. I'm discovering that when I calm down and give it a littlie time, my brain opens up and I am able to come up with more creative alternatives.

We are good to those around us…be good to ourselves too!

I have to admit I'm a little apprehensive about joining a support group. But I feel that the best people for me to talk with would be people who are living through the same stuff. I'll be okay I guess. Anything is better than what I'm going through. I hope I can get some help.

I have been involved with a Vietnam vet for the past six years. We've been on and off again the entire time. Last year I went to some classes at the VA to try to learn about PTSD. I already knew a lot about that because I also have a sister and brother-in-law who have been diagnosed with it. I went to the classes hoping to learn some coping skills for the relationship. I didn't really get any help with that. We just learned about the vets and the symptoms of the PTSD. I really need to talk with some people who are living with this and have learned how to do that.

I am at my wits' end. Again! I don't know what I'd do without being able to call someone. Someone else who understands. And cares. I really need my list of others in the support group and know I can call any time.

We're all here for a purpose and until He puts me somewhere else, I will rely on Him to help me.

Patience and love are empowering.

I have spent thirty-four years trying to find the secret, the magic pill for making this all work. We are both so tired. I'm finally realizing that it is more about the journey than the sprint. Now is not the time to quit, even though we both often feel like it. It's a lot of hard work, but it's worth it. Kind of like growing a garden. The good things do come along, but you just have to keep going, one day at a time. And I'm learning to take care of myself, and not just always be living for him and reacting to him. The more I do healthy things for me, the better we are. The better he is and the better I am able to be helpful when he needs it. I'm also really glad to be able to call my other vet wife friends and we can encourage each other. Lots of ups and downs but we're still going and I'm glad. Some days are good and some are not. But that's okay. Better to be alive than not.

We are not responsible for what we cannot control. A good thing to remind our vets too.

My father just passed away and I'm overwhelmed with all the stuff that goes with that, not to mention the grief. I have journaled off and on but not much recently. It's a very good thing for me to do during these days of grieving for Dad, as well as caring for Mom and a husband with PTSD. Every day is a struggle, not knowing if he will disappear, or wind up in the hospital again. I need to pay more attention to getting sleep and talking with others who can help.

✐

I would love to be able to talk to others who really understand what I'm going through.

✐

Periodically, I find myself agitated, depressed, and without energy. About two weeks ago, I was in a funk and suddenly overheard my internal monologue. I was shocked at how awful my own thoughts were! I forget that their PTSD really does affect us. I was thinking about how awful people are and how awful the world is and blah, blah, blah, negative, negative, negative. Pure poison. No wonder I was feeling so awful! I guess I've done it for so long I didn't even realize it anymore. So I decided I wanted to change that. I had the power to do something good for me!

I found two pretty little boxes and compiled two lists. One is a list of "random acts of kindnesses" and the other is a list of small enjoyable things I've been wanting to do but haven't found the time. I cut the lists into strips and placed them into their appropriate box. Every time I catch myself thinking negatively, I pull out a quick prayer from my prayer box (something I've used for a long time). Then I pull out a slip from one of the other two boxes. I make myself stop what I'm doing— and do what's on the slip of paper! So far, I've been able to turn dark, ugly thoughts into pots of tomato seedlings, donated purses, and shoes, to take to a nearby foster home for unwanted teenage girls (my closet is looking great!), learned two new recipes, got in touch with a friend I haven't talk to in a while, and adopted a grandparent at one of the several nearby nursing homes.

The dark thoughts seem to be getting better. I feel better. It may sound as if I'm not relying on God to help me with this, but I am. I just figure that He can't help me unless I'm willing to make an effort. At the expense of sounding crazy, I feel like He's helping me every day! And my vet and everyone else around me like the changes too.

I am finally learning to not feel responsible for everything about him and his happiness. I used to jump at every opportunity to try to keep him happy. I sort of lost myself in the process. My healthy self. My existence centered round his happiness or mood at the time. I found myself being afraid if his football team lost or if he got angry about anything I felt I could have prevented. Crazy, huh? I'm realizing now the value (for him and me) of him taking responsibility when he needs to and me not being too quick to think it's always my fault/problem. And he probably feels better and a little more grown up with me not hovering and smothering him. The healthier I get, the better it is for both of us. I know I'm getting better because his team lost yesterday and I was fine!

I'm learning to remember to really like being me!

Don't forget to pray, even if things seem to be going better. In the good times, it's easy to forget.

The most enlightening thing to me was the counselor's explanation of PTSD. It is from a once-in-a-lifetime traumatic event. Something terribly horrendously bad. For my vet it was witnessing the trauma numerous

192 Love Our Vets

times on a daily basis. He was the one who had to go back every day and put the bodies in the bags. Pieces and all. Even those who were his buddies. I cannot even imagine!

All of the social repercussions and odd reactions now make sense. He used to have a severe drinking problem and depression. Now there was a reason why. That makes it a little easier for me just to know. The more aware I am of his condition, the better I'm prepared for how he's going react. And the more compassion I feel toward him.

How do I take care of me? I keep myself busy. Places to go and things to do. He's content to just stay at home. He hides out because it is safe for him. But that would make me crazy. I love having my hobbies and part-time job. I love spending time with my grandchildren. I love singing in the choir. I don't ever want to feel housebound.

Another thing I've learned is to take separate cars when we do go somewhere together so he has the option of leaving early if he wants.

The hardest part has been his not wanting to be involved socially. I have to do things by myself or with friends or family, which is fine. I don't bug him about stuff anymore. There's something to be said for just accepting him as he is.

It has also been hard when he disconnects. I do feel lonely and a bit sad when he gets so depressed. At those times I need to get my support from other people and God.

I am a non-combat Vietnam veteran and also the father of a vet with PTSD. My son was deployed to Iraq, and like most men his age felt invincible. Benjie volunteered to go and wanted to be part of something bigger than himself. I don't know a lot of what happened to him over there, but as a non-combat vet, I know not to ask too probing questions about details of his experience. Many people want to know if they killed anyone, which would only aggravate the situation if it indeed happened.

The hardest part for me has been not being able to understand and share his pain of what he went through. Because we as parents didn't share a similar experience, the vet would not confide in a parent. This puts the parent in a position of being of no benefit to their son/daughter. From the father's position of trying to fix his hurting son, it's hard to realize that the only thing you can to is listen and accept what he/she has to say and then show unconditional love.

I've learned to become quiet and listen, not to offer fixes because I know it makes matters worse. I have to remind myself that my role now is not as his parent anymore but maybe a coach when he wants input. I don't take his negative emotions, of which there aren't many, personally.

Sometimes when things seem to have calmed down, I tend to forget about his struggles and then all of a sudden with an outbreak, it makes me take a step back and give him some space until he calms down. Benjie gets frustrated with others who don't live up to his own expectations. I attempt to get him to look at a bigger picture and give him a bigger perspective. I try to reason with him, but then I realize at this point in the episode that emotion is what's in control rather than reason. It's easier to reason with him after he has calmed down. It is also hard when he tends to withdraw and remove himself from those that love him.

On the positive side, all of this has given me perspective on life. It reminds me that I don't have control over many things and things happen for a reason—a reason I might not ever know. And that is okay. Also, I see a very tender heart in my son. He really wants to help the needy. And like many veterans, he sees injustice and would like to fix it but realizes that he can't do it alone. He has compassion for the Iraqi people and stays in touch with them.

Benjie has matured over the past year in many ways. He was admitted to inpatient treatment for seven weeks in a VA hospital in Colorado. In hindsight, I don't believe it was beneficial, and he actually returned in worse condition than when he left. After returning, he wanted a divorce. He didn't even move back home to see his children. He was angry.

But during this time many people were praying for him. After moving into two different apartments, he realized he was wrong and he returned to his wife. They are both doing so much better now and so are the children. I attribute this turnaround to God working in Benjie's life. A loving wife who demonstrated an unconditional love for him because of who she married, and not the way he behaved. She was not reactive in her emotions toward him but allowed God to work in her husband's life. She's an amazing woman who stayed with her husband through the difficult times. She has since been rewarded with a solid marriage and a loving home.

If I had to sum it all up, I would say that the key is to accept his situation as who he is now and love him even more with empathy, not pity.

$\mathscr{L}$❤

I've always been a bit shy, but if I can help just one person, even in a tiny way, to heal from and become stronger in spite of the PTSD, then I feel as if I've healed more myself.

Someone from Love Our Vets reached out to me, a total stranger, and held tight till I could regain my ground during the darkest time of my life. I don't want anyone to ever feel that they're all alone in this. It's a soul-stealing illness that, without love and support for the individual (and love and support for the supporter), can consume everything in its path.

$\mathscr{L}$❤

I used to always try to find the right answer when he was in a bad mood. The perfect thing to say. The ideal solution. But now I realize waiting until tomorrow helps. Sometimes a new day is better.

$\mathscr{L}$❤

I have also learned that after every war there is this PTSD. Now it is encouraging that the younger veterans can get help. It helps when they can connect with other vets.

It's not always about me. Although this morning it sure felt like it. As is typical, he had been up for hours before me, but today he was especially withdrawn. Mopey. Irritable. The first thing I noticed was that he was complaining about how cold it was (snowing outside!) yet he only wore a t-shirt. First frustration: I wanted to re-dress him or at least suggest that rather than complaining he put on something warmer. (Thankfully, I remembered that it is not my job to dress him or fix him.) Then he seemed to hover. Just like a lost puppy. Again, frustrating to me, a person who needs space, especially first thing in the morning. I was getting irritated, wanting to get on with my day, but feeling like I needed somehow to attend to him. I just wanted to run away, push him away or scream.

Thankfully my efforts at taking care of me are beginning to pay off. I was aware of my growing resentment and fears of feeling trapped, like he was robbing me of my life today. And I reminded myself (little pep talk) that I am free to take care of me, that I can love him *and* do what I must to meet my needs. Does not have to be either/or. I decided I could sit with him for a few minutes and then go forward with my day. And I am so glad I did.

It only took minutes for him to open up. He shared his nightmare. Dead bodies complete with horrific details. He felt like crying, yelling, and wondering what was so terribly wrong with him. I just held him. Reassured him of my love. Then, I strangely became aware of my own feelings paralleling his. That darn PTSD had gotten to both of us!

We held each other close. We talked. We cried. It was a precious time. Then he tearily said, "Of all the people, even veterans and counselors I have tried to talk to, you are the only one who really understands me. And loves me just the way I am."

Oh my. He touched me so deeply! What a tender precious moment. I was so ashamed of my earlier attitude. Why is it that the times we need each other the most we tend to pull away or push away?

Compassion heals. And the healing began in me.

The hardest part for me is to see how little he sleeps. How can he even function on so little sleep? I know it will affect his emotions and his health. And it's been so hard on me that we finally got beds in different rooms. It feels weird and I don't tell anyone. I miss not being able to snuggle during the night and in the morning, but at least I get sleep so I can function even if he cannot. We do make up for the cuddling at other times.

I found help from going to Al-Anon meetings. That was helpful in getting some coping mechanisms. Living with PTSD has a lot of similarities to living with an alcoholic. I'm doing so much better now.

There's a lot more to this PTSD thing than anyone realizes. It just doesn't make sense. It seems pretty hopeless at times. I could not keep on if I didn't have God.

It will never be perfect, but it can be good.

If I had known before what I know now about PTSD and all its craziness, I would do it all over again. Simply because I love my vet. And nothing in the world matters more to me.

Faith and love are stronger than PTSD.

⟪❧⟫

I can't tell you how the Love Our Vets-PTSD Family Support Group on Facebook saved my life and my son's life too! I live in Florida, and I got a call that he had tried to commit suicide at his base in Alaska. Of course I freaked out, as any mother would. Not knowing what to do I sent an urgent message to the Love Our Vets page. Thankfully, they immediately posted my question and amazing responses came pouring in! Lots of love, support and encouragement. And also practical help. Within two hours, someone had arranged a free flight for me to go to see him! And someone else who lived near the base offered for me to stay in her home! Wow. Thankfully, he is doing much better now, and so am I. Please surround yourself with good support, whether in person or on line…we do need each other!

⟪❧⟫

As Welby says, "It takes an exceptional person to love a warrior, especially a warrior whose war will never cease."

⟪❧⟫

With PTSD, every day is a victory!

GROUP DISCUSSION GUIDE

The true treasure of this book is that it gets to the heart of the loved ones. In addition to valuable practical help, it will provide a much needed catalyst in encouraging group participants to open up. It is in the personal application of the knowledge that true growth and healing will thrive.

The book is purposely designed to be read either cover to cover or randomly as needed. Its impact can be felt by both individuals as well as groups. After feeling the pulse of the group (each is unique), encourage them to all read the same section in preparation for the next meeting. Invite them to jot down notes and feelings and thoughts as they reflect on what they read. Some may not want any "homework." Assure them that this is purely voluntary. Just sitting in and observing and being with others will be beneficial. And encouraging. And comforting. But the more they can actively participate, the more they will get out of it. Also, remind them that everyone has something that will help the others.

A lot will depend on the time frame allotted for your group. If it is a class with start and finish dates, then it would work best to divide up the book accordingly. If the group is ongoing, you have the luxury of taking it as slowly as you wish. The material could take a long time to go through if you want.

Another variable will be the structure of your time in the session. If there is other material to be covered, then just part of the time can be allotted to this discussion. If this book is your primary resource, then there is quite a bit of flexibility.

The following are some ideas to encourage discussion. As a group facilitator, I hope you will feel free to draw upon your expertise and intuition. There is no one right way to do this. Just a few ideas to get the ball rolling. Ideally it might be good to tap into all three sections at each meeting. Something from Part One, Part Two, and Part Three. Part Two will go the quickest, but is perhaps the most important. I encourage you to revisit that section as an ongoing reminder each time you meet.

$\mathcal{L}$❧

Section One

Reaffirm: Our Questions
Go through each question, perhaps one or more at each meeting, and discuss. Encourage responses to these questions:

What did you feel as you read this?
What did you learn?
Is this something you struggle with?
What can you add?
Do you have experiences to share that will be helpful to others?

$\mathcal{L}$❧

Section Two

Replenish: Our Needs
Focus on one of the twenty-one needs or more if time allows. Help the group honestly assess which areas are the weakest and how to grow in those. Encourage them to share stories and examples of how they're implementing these good things in their lives. Also, it is helpful to invite each person to relate where they could use help and see what others are doing that works for them.

꧁

SECTION THREE

Reflect: Our Wisdom

This section affords a wide variety of input. Feel free to cover as many segments as time allows, taking care to camp on each one long enough to really absorb and reflect. There will be a great variation in which testimonials spark more discussion than others. These quotes are a wonderful springboard for discussion. Invite personal responses, providing safety for emoting. At the end, try to always bring it back to the positive. What can we do? We can be empowered as long as we have hope.

HELP FOR TIMES OF TRANSITION

WHY MILITARY FAMILIES SHOULD BE PREPARED FOR PTSD

The one you tearfully bid farewell may never be in your arms again—at least not like you remember them. Whether or not your service member has directly experienced combat, he or she could come home with post-traumatic stress (PTS), or even Posttraumatic Stress Disorder (PTSD).

You've probably heard of PTSD before, but did you know that any-one who has been through a very stressful event likely feels some level of PTS? It could be as common as a car wreck or as intense as combat. The difference between the two is how it impacts your life. It's normal to feel a bit jumpy about driving down the freeway if you were hit the last time you did it. But when that jumpy feeling starts interrupting your normal day, or even your night, you may be dealing with an entirely dif-ferent beast: PTSD.

Your service member is no different. When someone experiences combat, he or she will probably feel the impact of that stress afterward. But when that stress morphs into something that takes over their life or is uncontrollable, you'll need to get help.

Are you prepared?

You probably think right now that this lady is crazy and none of this applies to you or your warrior. This kind of stuff only happens to other people. But if your service member has seen combat, you may join the world of other people. And wouldn't it better to be ready for it?

The good news is that there is hope. I know because my veteran and I are living it every day. But there was a time when we both were ready to throw in the towel. We thought we couldn't do it anymore. Looking back, we are so glad we stuck it out. We both got help. And today neither of us would trade the other for the world, even with the PTSD.

Here are three things that have helped me and many others to prepare for the wonderful homecoming of our heroes and to increase the odds of a fulfilling relationship in spite of the possibility of PTSD.

1. LEARN ALL THAT YOU CAN ABOUT PTSD—NOW. I had never heard of it when I met my husband. (PTSD? What is that, a radio station?) If your loved one has been exposed to potentially traumatic events, it may be helpful to educate yourself about what you could be dealing with. I found a helpful class through the VA for families and spouses. I also read all I could get at online. I learned what to look for, such as nightmares, flashbacks, hyper-vigilance, outbursts of rage, anxiety, substance abuse, withdrawal, or even suicidal thoughts, to name a few. Another good place to check out is the Coaching into Care programs through the VA. (See www.LoveOurVets.org for more resources.)

2. CONNECT WITH OTHERS WHO ARE LIVING SUCCESSFULLY WITH PTSD. Be prepared to meet for coffee with another spouse, or connect with other loved ones on Facebook pages such as LOVE OUR VETS - PTSD FAMILY SUPPORT, LLC. Knowing where to find others who are going through the same thing will make you feel relieved that you are not alone. You are not crazy, and neither is your loved one. People share openly about their struggles, and also what helps them. (See www.LoveOurVets.org for Support Network information).

3. KNOW HOW TO TAKE GOOD CARE OF YOU AND YOUR NEEDS. I wasted so many days at the doctor's office, trying to fix what I thought were imbalanced hormones! Several meltdowns and a broken foot later (don't ask), I starting paying attention to my needs and issues. I try to remember that it is not all about taking care of him, and that I also need to take care of me. When I do that we both benefit.

If you take time to put these three things in place as precautions before your warrior comes home, your chances of a happily ever after will be much greater.

For a more comprehensive and ongoing list of support links and resources, visit www.LoveOurVets.org

$\mathscr{L}$❦

VICARIOUS TRAUMA

By Amanda Juza, MSW
Co-facilitator of Vet Center Family PTSD Education Classes

As PTSD begins to invade your home, you may feel as though you are slowly losing control of your own emotions. A place that may have once been safe to express insecurities, doubt, and concern has now become a war zone in and of itself. When someone you care about has experienced trauma, you carry a little of that trauma with you as well.

In the treatment of PTSD (Posttraumatic Stress Disorder), unfortunately many practitioners don't look past the veterans themselves. Not much research has been completed regarding the impact PTSD has on families and intimate relationships. Many organizations such as the Department of Defense and the Department of Veteran Affairs are just beginning to explore the warrior/veteran as a whole person, with a family and other external factors that influence their ability to perform the mission. The United States Army launched a new program in 2009 called the Master Resiliency course. This course is designed to view the soldier as a whole person that is impacted by their environment. The field of social work would describe this as the systems theory that integrated a person into their environment. This theory looks at not just the soldier but how family stressors impact their ability to perform the duties necessary on the battlefield.

Another element of the person-in-environment concept is to look at how the warrior/veteran has impacted their home environment. Many military units provide training for families while the units are deployed to combat. This training discusses the psychological impact and symptoms their veteran may experience when they return home from a combat zone. What does this mean for current active-duty spouses? Well, it means there is hope, hope for education, training, and understanding, not just for the warrior, but for the family as well.

As PTSD affects your family, you just want to cry. The feelings are overwhelming. It's no longer safe to cry. When you cry, he feels even more helpless, and the tension in the home just increases. With every week, it feels that your words of concern are met with anger and frustration. This leaves you feeling hopeless, then angry and frustrated.

This is vicarious trauma. When someone you care about has experienced trauma, you carry a little of that trauma with you as well. So how do you work through the trauma? The first step is to understand your own risk factors for trauma. Spend some time looking at your childhood: Did you grow up in a household with PTSD? You may not have known it at the time, but hindsight being 20/20, you might see some of your father's behavior of hypervigilance and angry outbursts as some of his own PTSD. Knowing your own personal trauma history is really important. You may realize that, as your veteran learns about his or her trauma triggers, you may have some as well. It's important for you to recognize that some of your veteran's behavior may be triggering some of your own trauma. Here is a list of questions you should ask yourself, to determine what trauma triggers you might have:

1. What is my personality type? (aggressive, passive, submissive)
2. How do I cope with stress? (Is this a healthy reaction?) For example, do I run to the local drive-through for some comfort food, or do I participate in thirty minutes of exercise?
3. Have I experienced trauma in my life?
4. What are some current stressors in my life? An example might be that you may have just retired or started a new job. A lifestyle change such as this can add stress to your life.
5. Where do I get my social support? Do you have someone you could call that is willing to lend a supportive hand, or even a listening ear?
6. What are my spiritual resources? What are your spiritual beliefs,

and do you connect with others who share your beliefs?

The second step is to look at what signs and symptoms you may be experiencing. Is your world changing? Sometimes when PTSD enters your life slowly, these changes are so subtle that you may have to look back five, ten, or even fifteen years. Some key questions to ask yourself would be, have my views about the world changed? Look at any physical or emotional changes. Have you noticed a drastic decrease or increase in your weight or even in your energy levels? Are you finding that you are also short-tempered, or quick to become angry? Other relationships in your life may have changed also. All of these could be signs and symptoms that you are experiencing vicarious trauma.

The good news is that there is hope. Do all you can to get support for yourself, while your vet gets the support he needs. Give yourself permission to learn and grow and not be surprised by the feelings you will experience as a result of this vicarious trauma.

LIVING ON TSUNAMI ISLAND

On March 11, 2011, the island of Japan was struck by a surprise tsunami. In addition to total devastation, there were several nuclear reactors on the brink of explosion.

Living with a veteran with PTSD has some similarities to living on an island. As beautiful as it is, there is always the threat of a tsunami. In thinking through the parallels, I offer a few steps that will help us survive in the event of a sudden storm that hits with no warning.

1. The first thing to do is prepare. Have a plan, and be ready for it. How will I take care of me? (call a friend, go for a drive or a walk, go to my special room in the house, do a craft, etc.)
2. Know the warning signs. What are his triggers? What are mine? Be aware of what is happening in my body and my feelings.
3. Keep myself safe. Practice assertiveness and healthy boundaries. Stick up for myself without attacking him.
4. Nuclear containment: Contain my rage that may get triggered. Know my power to keep it from escalating. Now is a good time to ask for God's help. Don't fight. Have a healthy outlet for my reaction, rather than adding to the explosion.
5. Let time work. It's like a tidal wave for him…when it crashes it is extremely intense! But no wave continues to keep its intensity forever. He will calm down. The storm passes. Be prepared for aftershocks. Take the time to talk about it another time, after all is calm.
6. Finally, remember *he* (the vet we love) is not the tsunami. He is a victim of it just like we are. Ultimately, love and compassion win the day.

A PRAYER A DAY

Through the years, many of us have experienced the comfort and help that comes from prayer. In fact, some of us could not survive without it. Wherever you are on your spiritual journey, prayer is always an option. It is an opening of the heart, just coming as you are. To the One who cares and can help.

The following are some suggested prayers we have found helpful. There are no special words one needs, just honest baring of the soul. Sometimes you just need to cry in His presence, or weep, or beg, or give thanks. To help make things simpler, there are thirty-one prayers here, one for each day of the month. The pattern is set up for couples, but the principles apply to any family members and loved ones too. God will take all prayers!

DAY 1

Dear God,
Please help me with everything I need today. Please help him too. Increase our love for each other.

DAY 2

Dear God,
Would you open my heart to be more compassionate? Help him know he is loved. Open our eyes to Your blessings today.

DAY 3

Dear God,
Please remind me that I cannot fix everything. Help him relax today. Bless us with peace.

DAY 4

Dear God,
Give me strength for today. Please give him hope today. And God, please remind us that we are not the enemy.

DAY 5

Dear God,
Fill me with gratitude. Please help him see the good things around him. Please help us appreciate all the good people in our lives.

DAY 6

Dear God,
Please flow Your love through me. Please help him receive that love. Help us hug each other more today.

DAY 7

Dear God,
Please show me what I need today just for me. Help him be okay when I take care of me. Help us sleep well tonight.

DAY 8

Dear God,
Please help me learn something new today. Help him learn something new today too. Please help us not be afraid to grow.

DAY 9

Dear God,
Please help me connect with someone special today. Help him connect with a special person too. Help us have healthy relationships.

DAY 10

Dear God,
I need to laugh today. Help me lighten up. Help him laugh today too. Bless us with joy.

DAY 11

Dear God,
I need wisdom. Help him in his decision-making too. Help us be a good team together.

DAY 12

Dear God,
Help me to see what is truly important and to let go of what is not. Help him also to see what really matters and to let go of what does not. Help us together to value what really matters.

DAY 13

Dear God,
Please help me accept him as he is, totally and unconditionally. Help him accept me as I am, totally and unconditionally. Help us appreciate each other's strengths.

DAY 14

Dear God,
Please give me self-control when I need it. Please give him self-control also. Help us both make healthy choices.

DAY 15

Dear God,
Please help me see things from an eternal perspective. Help him also see things that way. Let us focus on what really matters in the long run and not get fooled by things that ultimately do not matter.

DAY 16

Dear God,
Please give me strength on the inside to be victorious over all the challenges that come today. Help him feel strong in the inside instead of afraid. Help us both be strong together, leaning on You.

DAY 17

Dear God,
Help me look beyond today to a brighter tomorrow. Help him to not think so much about death but about life. Help us remember that You are our source of life.

DAY 18

Dear God,
Help me remember that life is a journey, not a race. Help him to walk through this day with hope. Bless us with wisdom and tranquility.

DAY 19

Dear God,
Help me stay grounded with all the ups and downs of this day. I pray that he will find his stability in You and not be toppled by mood swings. Bless us with peace today.

DAY 20

Dear God,
Help me be the wife he needs. Help him be the husband I need. And for all that we lack, please be everything to us both that we need.

DAY 21

Dear God,
Help me to express my needs graciously. Help him to hear me. And help us be able to communicate openly and lovingly.

DAY 22

Dear God,
I am so weary. Pleae help me drawn comfort and strength from You. Help him find blessing in showing me love. Help us stay tuned to each other's needs.

DAY 23

Dear God,

Help me surround myself with good people and wise input. Help him do the same. May we both be positive influences on each other.

DAY 24

Dear God,

Help me make healthy choices in what I eat and drink today. Help him eat and drink what he needs today too. Help us see and reap the benefits of making these good choices.

DAY 25

Dear God,

Help me forgive. Help him also to forgive. We need to remember that forgiving is mostly for our own good, to not let that bitterness eat away at us.

DAY 26

Dear God,

Help me use all the gifts and abilities you have endowed me with. Help him see that he has purpose in life too. Help us together to bring blessing to others.

DAY 27

Dear God,

Help me not become buried in my own self-pity. Help him also to see that others have pain too. Remind us to give thanks for all the goodness we do have.

DAY 28

Dear God,

Help me let go of unrealistic expectations of others. Help him also to not expect perfection. Help us focus on learning and the value of the process of life itself.

DAY 29

Dear God,

I want to feel good today. Help me to fill all my senses with good things and to enjoy it. Help him to allow himself to feel good and to see beauty. Open our awareness to all the joys that are at our disposal.

DAY 30

Dear God,

Help me be aware of my own anxieties and triggers. Help him become more aware of his too. And as we become more attentive, help us to avoid saying or doing hurtful things that we would regret.

DAY 31

Dear God,

Help me cherish the man You have given to me. Help him cherish me. And may we both continue on our journey in becoming all You intended us to be inn spite of the challenges of life.

DAILY PRAYER

Dear God,

Help me remember that my vet is Your child. You have put me here to love him, not fix him. Help me love him today, and entrust him into Your capable hands. May we both find all we need in You.

I Loved Someone with PTSD

By Welby O'Brien

I loved someone with PTSD...
Had no clue how hard it could be.
Was I the only one who knew
What PTSD could put you through?

If only I knew just what to say,
Or just tried harder to make his day.
Was it me or was it him?
What was this darkness that stole him away?

I cry alone. It hurts so much.
He cannot seem to feel my touch.
Where does he go behind that wall,
Or in that cave so dark and small?

His pain is abysmal, locked deep inside.
All he knows is how to hide.
The horrors of war forever torment
This man I love, and won't relent.

I'm all alone, afraid and torn,
Feel so tired, weary, worn.
Please, God, show me what to do
To help us both to make it through!

I'm NOT alone, it came to me.
Faith and love can set me free.
Prayers of help, and people who know,
My lifelines of hope to help me grow.

It isn't him. It isn't me.
It's only the cruel PTSD.
Though always there, we don't have to be numb,
If we just take one day at a time.

I love someone with PTSD,
And I am sure that he loves me.
The pain and struggles we'll fight each day,
My love for him is here to stay.

I loved someone with PTSD,
And I'm so glad he's here with me.
Although it is not always fun
It's the best thing I have ever done!